ABOUT THE AUTHOR

Tarot, oracles, and magic have all influenced Barbara's life for more than a decade. She has studied under some of the most influential tarot experts in the world and continues to teach and work with some of the brightest stars in the field.

Barbara enjoys the challenge of giving a voice to tarot cards and oracle decks. She has had the good fortune to write books for several decks, including *A Guide to Mystic Faerie Tarot (Mystic Faerie Tarot)*, *The Gilded Tarot Companion (The Gilded Tarot)*, *The Witchy Tarot (The Hip Witch Kit)*, and *The Dreamer's Journal (Mystic Dreamer Tarot)*.

Photo by Joshua Masiker; background by Julie Fain

DESTINY'S PORTAL

ABOUT THE ARTIST

Mythic fantasy artist Jessica Galbreth lives in Ohio with her husband and their two children. She studied fine art, with a major in painting, for three years at the Toledo Museum of Art. Jessica is perhaps most celebrated for her ability to capture the haunting, often mysterious beauty of goddesses and fairies from mythology.

In 1999, Jessica began her art career with a modest website. Now you can find her work globally in numerous formats, including prints, greeting cards, calendars, books, and collectible figurines and ceramics.

BARBARA MOORE

DESTINY'S PORTAL

CARD ARTWORK BY
JESSICA GALBRETH

Llewellyn Publications
Woodbury, Minnesota

FIRST EDITION
First Printing, 2008

Book design and editing by Rebecca Zins
Cover design by Kevin R. Brown
Llewellyn is a registered trademark of Llewellyn Worldwide, Ltd.

978-0-7387-1410-3
This book is a component of the *Enchanted Oracle* kit,
which consists of a boxed kit of 36 full-color cards,
a fairy charm, a card pouch, and this perfect-bound book.

Llewellyn Worldwide does not participate in, endorse, or have any authority or responsibility concerning private business transactions between our authors and the public.

All mail addressed to the author is forwarded but the publisher cannot, unless specifically instructed by the author, give out an address or phone number.

Any Internet references contained in this work are current at publication time, but the publisher cannot guarantee that a specific location will continue to be maintained. Please refer to the publisher's website for links to authors' websites and other sources.

Llewellyn Publications
A Division of Llewellyn Worldwide, Ltd.
2143 Wooddale Drive, Dept. 978-0-7387-1410-3
Woodbury, MN 55125-2989
www.llewellyn.com

Printed in the United States of America

Acknowledgments

A special thank-you to Jessica Galbreth for creating such inspiring art. A grateful and humble thank-you to Becky, who makes my words sound so good and who designs the prettiest books ever.

—B. M.

Special thanks to Barbara Moore, whose insight into the deeper meanings of the tarot was crucial for the success of this project.

—J. G.

Barbara and Jessica both wish to thank Llewellyn's fine production team for making such a perfect package for our work. Becky, Kevin, Wendy, Lynne, and Nanette, great job!

Dedication

To Lisa, for her own quiet magic.

—B. M.

To my husband, Josh, for giving me wings to fly with, yet keeping my feet firmly planted on the ground when I need it most.

—J. G.

CONTENTS

The Cards 13

Author's Note

Throughout this text, I use phrases like nature, the universe, and the goddess when I am referring to the concept of a higher being. Sometimes I will say "the universe, the goddess, or whatever deity you honor." In all these cases, please take it to mean whatever power or deity you acknowledge and honor.

Within this book, you'll find enchantments for charging your fairy charm with your power (that is, your intent and will), making prayers to the universe, and casting spells. Various supplies are suggested, such as crystals, stones, candles, ribbons, and essential oils. The supplies used are based on magical properties that are recognized by many magical practitioners. However, feel free to make substitutions and make these enchantments your own. For example, there are many oils associated with passion or healing. I picked ones that work for me; you may prefer other ones. Always check for sensitivity when using a new oil.

If you don't have access to a variety of supplies, keep in mind that white (for candles and ribbons) is always appropriate. Quartz crystals can be used in place of other crystals and stones. Sandalwood is also a generally useful oil and incense.

You should, of course, feel free to re-create any of the chants, spells, or prayers in your own words.

Finally, nothing in this book is meant to replace common sense or professional legal or medical (physical, mental, or emotional) advice.

ARTIST'S NOTE

This deck features my very favorite paintings that I've done over the years as a professional artist, and even a few created just for this project. So many requests have been made of me to put my work together for a deck. Until recently, I didn't feel I was ready or that it was time. A chance meeting with the folks at Llewellyn came at the perfect time. As we began excitedly talking about the prospect of an oracle deck featuring my art, I knew that the stars had aligned and that the timing was finally right.

I worked mainly with watercolors to create the pieces used in this oracle deck. Each piece really is like a special journey for me. I start out with a vague idea of what I am trying to create and then let the deity in the painting take on a life and personality of her own. After I finish a painting, which normally takes me about a full week from start to finish, I am only temporarily satisfied. Soon, a new seed of an idea is planted in my mind, and I cannot rest until I begin again.

Barbara has done a wonderful job interpreting my artwork for this project. She has perfectly captured the mood I was trying to convey with each piece and has noted all the symbols and their relevance. I truly feel that this oracle deck and book interweaves the magic of each image with a sense of deep knowledge and enlightenment. It is my sincere hope that you enjoy this deck as much as Barbara and I have enjoyed putting it together and bringing it to fruition.

WELCOME TO THE
ENCHANTED ORACLE

*S*eek your destiny through trailing vines and gnarled trees
to a secret realm rich with myth and magic. An enchanted place awaits, filled with ethereal fairies and haunting
deities. Here sorceresses wield their spells. And it is here
where you, surrounded by power and bathed in the glow
of the moon, can weave your future.

Your life is a gift, and you can make of it what you
will. Here you will find knowledge, skills, and tools that
will help you craft the magical life of your dreams. Using
the influential energies of nature and your own inherent

power, you can transform yourself and, to a certain extent, your circumstances.

Within the *Enchanted Oracle,* you will discover thirty-six images that do so much more than simply reveal destinies. You will find the power to create your future. Most people use an oracle as a fortune-telling device, but an oracle is much more than that. An oracle, properly used, is a means of receiving messages from the divine and a place for divine communication. It's true that you can request glimpses of the future, insofar as it is known. You can also seek guidance in any situation and create influences that can shape the future. These applications are exciting, and used in conjunction with peeks at the future, they open up worlds of possibilities.

Within these pages, you will learn how to use the cards, the fairy charm, and sometimes other items (such as candles or crystals) to create your own enchanted world. In that world, you will find your own magic and use it to enchant your life, for to *enchant* something is to use magical influence upon it or to endow it with magical properties. You will certainly magically influence your life, and you will endow the charm with magical properties. Through all of your experiences and practices, never forget that the magic is within you—that it is a result of your will and your focus combined with the energies of the universe.

In the pages that follow, as you explore the myths and magic of goddesses, fairies, and sorceresses, you will find much to delight and inspire. You will find answers. You will find guidance. You will find possibilities. You will find the goddess, fairy, and sorceress within yourself.

Enjoy the journey.

HOW TO USE
THE ENCHANTED ORACLE

The *Enchanted Oracle* can be used in a variety of ways to add magic to your daily life. First and foremost, it is a card deck oracle. Using the cards, you can perform readings to get advice, discover answers, and gain insight into many questions you may have. You'll learn how to use the cards in this way starting on page 3.

However, card deck oracles are notoriously ineffective for yes or no questions. A pendulum is much more useful in seeking such knowledge. The enclosed fairy charm is meant to serve several purposes, one of which is being used as a pendulum; pages 2–3 explain how.

1

Magic can be added to your life by spells, enchantments, and visualizations. The cards are well suited to these activities, which you can use if the card comes up in a reading. Or, if you have a specific need, you can look at the list starting on page 10, find one that meets your need, and use it without performing a reading. Journaling suggestions are also included, as writing is an excellent path to self-discovery and wisdom.

Using a Pendulum

The mechanics of using a pendulum are very simple. The most challenging part is learning to clear your mind so that you get a clear reading. Set your intent on receiving an answer from the universe, not a reflection of what you want to hear.

Sit at a table with arms and legs uncrossed. Hold your pendulum in your dominant hand by grasping the clasp between your thumb and first two fingers. Rest your elbow on the table and hold your hand at an almost 90-degree angle to your wrist. Your thumb is parallel with the table. Angle your arm so that the fairy is about two to four inches from the table.

Clear your mind. Ask a series of yes or no questions that you know the answers to, and watch how the pendulum moves. This is how you learn how your pendulum responds. Usually, but not always, a pendulum moves vertically or horizontally for yes and no, and moves in circles to indicate that the answer is unknown or it's not for you to know at this time. Keep practicing until you get consistent results.

See the list starting on page 10 for specific pendulum techniques.

Divination with the Cards

Using the *Enchanted Oracle*, you will discover and use your magic in a variety of ways. The most popular use is, of course, divining the future. Fear of the unknown is one of the most unsettling experiences for many people. It makes sense, then, that people would want to eliminate that anxiety by eliminating the unknown. How often do you find yourself waiting for a decision or event, thinking, "I don't care how it turns out; I just want the waiting over"? At those times, you will want very much to use this oracle for divination.

One of the weaknesses in seeking knowledge of the future is that it often can't be known. In so many cases, the future isn't set in stone, so no oracle can predict it absolutely. Think of your local weather forecast. The forecast for the next day is often pretty accurate. The three-day forecast is less so. The ten-day forecast…well, we all know how accurate that is. The reason is that there are so many variables involved in creating the weather that a change in any one of them affects the whole picture. When a weather system is very active is when you most want a forecast, yet it is during those times that it is most difficult to make an accurate prediction. Your life is probably even more complex than the weather, and you are most likely to seek your future when your life is "active"—that is, when things are very much up in the air and you are feeling uncertain.

Useful divination is possible. Understanding what you can accomplish goes a long way toward eliminating frustration or inaccurate predictions. Divination is the art of discovering what is hidden and revealing potentials. When you are divining about a situation, you can see probable futures. Patterns will reveal themselves. Underlying causes and effects will become apparent. You will find this knowledge incredibly useful. Once you see the direction of a situation, you can also see how you can encourage or change that direction. If you cannot change it, you can learn how to prepare for it. Once you have divined a situation, you can best employ your magic and do your part to weave your future.

To aid in divination, each card has an oracle message. These cards are not designed to be read upside down. If a card is reversed, simply turn it right-side up.

STEPS FOR PERFORMING A DIVINATION

1. Decide on your question, and write it down.
2. Select the spread you are going to use.
3. Shuffle the cards.
4. Lay out the cards according to the spread you selected.
5. Interpret the cards.
6. Write out the reading in your journal.

Spreads

A spread is simply the way that you lay out the cards on the table (or whatever surface you are working on). The positions for the cards are usually numbered, indicating the order in which you lay them down, and named, describing the way the card should be read. For example, a card in a position named "the past" pertains to your past.

ONE-CARD SPREADS

The easiest and often the most effective spreads for the *Enchanted Oracle* are one-card spreads. The number of one-card spreads is infinite, because you can draw one card to answer virtually any question you may have. Many people like to draw a card every day for advice to take with them as they move through their day.

Here are some tried and true one-card spreads.

1. What do I need to know about _____?
2. In achieving my goal, what is my best next step?
3. What will happen if _____?
4. I'm feeling confused. How can I clarify my feelings?

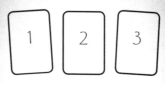

Three-Card Spread

1: This is leaving you

2: This is here now

3: This is coming toward you

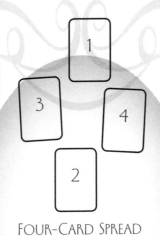

FOUR-CARD SPREAD

1: This is what you need to take with you

2: This is what you need to leave behind you

3: This is your next step

4: This is the probable outcome

List of Spells, Enchantments, Visualizations, Pendulum Use, and Journaling Exercises

TRANSFORMATION

YOUR BODY

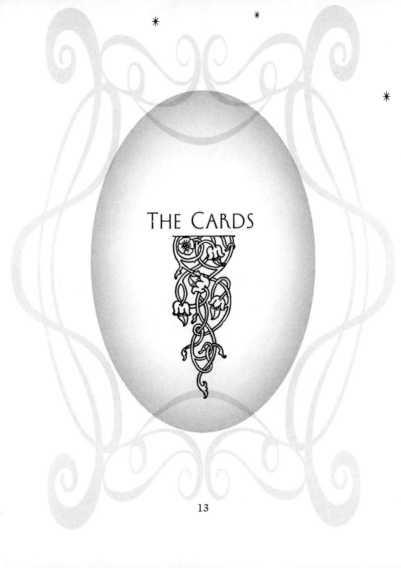

THE CARDS

Autumn Splendor

Cool, brisk air. Trees painting gold, red, and orange leaves against an impossibly clear blue sky. Red, sweet apples bursting with life and flavor. Dark green zucchinis, shiny red tomatoes, and bright orange pumpkins everywhere. What could be a better representation of accomplishment than Nature at harvest time?

After months of nurturing, growing, and tending, it's time to reap the harvest. At this time, Nature bedecks herself in, some say, her most gorgeous array, as if in celebration of her own accomplishment. So it is with us, isn't it? After working hard, planning every detail, making corrections and adjustments, redoing, assessing, and tweaking, we might feel a justified sense of pride. We'd like people to see what we've done and to praise both the finished product and our careful efforts in creating it. Even though we know what we've done is worthy, somehow it feels more real if there is some sort of public acknowledgment, whether formal or informal.

Our Autumn Splendor fairy is a subtle but potent representation of pride following a job well done. With their red and orange hues, her richly colored garments exude energy, vitality, passion, focus, and harvest. The leaves in her hair indicate that her actions and accomplishments are in her thoughts; she is very conscious of them. The spirals adorning her and the background are signs that everything is and has gone with the flow of Nature, that everything is just as it should be. The tiny crescent near her eye is not quite full; a little something is still lacking. Perhaps she wants external acknowledgment. But notice she is not overtly seeking it. She looks rather shyly over her shoulder, unwilling to demand or ask for a compliment but nonetheless hoping that anyone seeing her splendor will indeed say something pleasant.

Oracle Message

Your splendor is showing! You have accomplished something wonderful, and you are understandably proud. And you should be. But the act of accomplishment isn't the focus here. With this card, you are being asked about how you react afterwards. Do you want recognition? Are you getting it—in particular, are you getting it from the person, people, or institution that matters most to you? Are you responding graciously to any acknowledgment? Or, on a less pleasant note, are you demanding attention? Don't ruin a perfectly splendid achievement by draping it with arrogance. Surround it instead with the sparkle of grace and quiet, confident pride.

Thank-You Notes

Just as you desire a little recognition for your achievements, don't forget to acknowledge the universe, the gods and goddesses, or whatever deities you honor. Throughout your project you relied on them for inspiration, guidance, and strength. Take a few minutes to send a bit of gratitude their way.

If you like, before starting this little ritual, make a list of any specific inspirations or guidance that you are grateful for. Then light a white candle and say:

> *You were there at the start*
> *I give thanks from my heart*
> *You were there at the end*
> *All my love I do send.*

If you made a list, you can give thanks for each item, then repeat the verse. When you are done, snuff out the candle.

BEWITCHING

Bewitched, beguiled—who hasn't felt like something or someone has cast a spell over them? It can be a scary, exciting time, when you hardly feel in control of your actions or feelings. Or perhaps you don't enjoy being bewitched—feeling like someone or something else is controlling you.

Or perhaps it is you who has bewitched someone else. Having that power over someone or something can be scary and exciting, too. Quite a bit of responsibility comes with that power. It is better, more responsible and safer, to bewitch yourself and your life. The ability to bewitch can be harnessed and used consciously. You can do it and enjoy the results of your own focused intent and magic. And you can guard against becoming bewitched yourself. You can be the writer of your destiny.

In Bewitching, we see a young, powerful witch. Around her head, she wears the symbol of the moon, showing the moon in all its phases: waxing, full, and waning. Resting on her head, this symbol shows her focus and intent. She carries a pentagram, a symbol of the four elements: earth, water, air, and fire. The top point represents spirit, which rules all the elements. The pentacle in her hand indicates using her focus and intent to manifest change in the physical world. This is, in essence, the nature of magic. She is smart to be clothed in black, the color of protection and of the crone goddess. Magic can be dangerous if misused, so a bit of protection and the wisdom of the crone goddess will be useful. For while this witch is smart and powerful, she lacks experience, so the ancient wisdom of the crone will serve her well. It seems she is willing to heed the crone's wisdom, because a raven, a messenger from the spiritual realm, is on its way to her. The crescent moon shows that not all is revealed—that she doesn't know everything and is wise to seek advice before casting her spell.

Oracle Message

The power, knowledge, and wisdom you seek are all available to you. You can certainly accomplish what you wish. Use your abilities wisely, or there will be unforeseen consequences. Seek the advice of someone more experienced than you before implementing your plan, whether it is a spell, project, or course of action. Remember that with power comes responsibility. If you are planning a bit of magic, keep in mind this practice of many witches. It is a kind of "out" clause to keep you from causing harm you don't intend. At the end of a spell, say something like, "I ask for this or something better, for the greater good of all, and with harm to none. So mote it be."

Call the Raven

If you are thinking of casting a spell, starting a project, or taking a course of action, take some time to assess the wisdom of it. Think everything through and try to imagine various scenarios that could occur. Try to pinpoint any areas where unintended consequences could result.

While using logic, reason, and experience is a good start, sometimes there are facts that you just can't be aware of or effects that you didn't consider. This is an important time to consult the spiritual realm, through the universe, the goddess, or any deity you honor.

Write out your intention on a small piece of paper. Put a black candle in a fireproof bowl or plate, and light it. Burn frankincense incense to enhance meditation and receptiveness to the spirit realm. Light the paper with the candle, and let it burn in the plate or bowl. As the smoke floats up, say:

24

Raven wise, raven dear
Voice of the crone
I wish to hear
Advise me, please,
With a message clear.

Sit comfortably with your feet on the ground, or if you prefer, lie down in a room where you will not be interrupted. Close your eyes and imagine a raven coming to you, ready to share the wisdom of the universe regarding your plans. Ask it if your plan is sound and if there is anything you need to know before you commence. Stay and meditate with this image until you understand the answer. Thank the raven and the universe for their wisdom, open your eyes, and snuff out the candle.

CELTIC WITCH

Do you live a life woven with magic? Or do you know someone who lives such a charmed life? What would such a life look like?

How do you define magic? At its most basic, magic is the application of intent to create change in the world. If it's so simple, then, why do we use all the symbols, candles, incantations, and other mystical tools and trappings? All of these things help to focus our mind and our intent. Symbols, like words, are filled with power, sometimes very ancient and strong power. By their nature, symbols trigger a response deep in the human psyche. They help activate our connection with power, the power inherent within us all and the power available within the universe. You

27

can use symbols to increase your own magic and weave it throughout every aspect of your life. Even mundane, day-to-day activities can sparkle with magic. Sounds like a pretty nice way to experience life, doesn't it?

Our Celtic Witch embodies a life woven with magic. The Celts filled their lives with intricate and beautiful symbols. Behind our witch is an elaborate Celtic knot, showing the complexity and interconnectedness of the universe. It reminds us that magic is in everything. Around her head is an odd symbol that echoes another ancient magical tradition: the scarab was a symbol of creation in Egyptian magic. It is an appropriate symbol for a headpiece, signifying that by focusing her mind, she can create change in the world. She wears a pentagram, representing the elements (earth, water, fire, and air) and spirit, again showing how intent or will in harmony with spirit can influence the mundane elements. The various spiral and knot tattoos acknowledge the importance of the connectedness of all life and the cycles of nature. She carries a red candle, representing passion, fire, and the mother goddess from whom all creation comes.

Oracle Message

It is time to imbue your life with magic... tap into your power... plug in to the universe. There is so much available to you. Notice signs and symbols around you; what kinds of power or magic are they hinting at? How can you share that magic? Research magical and historical symbols. Discover one that represents what you are seeking and that resonates with your soul. Find ways to sprinkle that symbol throughout your daily life to inspire and encourage you. Draw it on a piece of paper and stick it to your mirror so you see it every morning. Find a piece of jewelry that incorporates it. Make a cover for your journal that includes it. Make a cake and draw the symbol into the frosting. Do whatever you can to focus your mind and intent to help create the change and make the magic you desire.

Cernunnos

We spend much of our energy controlling our behavior, thoughts, and actions. It seems that we use our logic and reason to control our emotions and, to an even larger extent, our instincts.

It is true that the world would probably be a scary place if everyone followed every instinct all the time. While too many rules, regulations, and social mores can be stifling and repressive, having some makes the world a much nicer place to exist. But there are times when acknowledging and indulging our primal urges can be good. If we cut ourselves off entirely from our ancient ties to the earth and nature, we lose an important connection that feeds our

31

soul and inspires our mind. Our connection with the earth and nature is ultimately spiritual. However, earth and nature are physical, as are we. It is normal that our connection is enhanced and celebrated with physical activities. Through our five senses, we have lots of ways to enjoy this connection. And really, how much of an excuse do you need to indulge in some sensuous decadence?

Cernunnos is an ancient Celtic god. He has many titles: the horned god, the lord of the hunt, and Pan. Here, he is honored as the lord of wild things. He is a god of nature and fertility. He is the epitome of primal essence. He is all things physical. He is also a shaman and a shapeshifter. His experience and understanding of the physical world enhance and empower his connection with the spiritual world. We see all of this in this card: the ancient forest, the animals, his antlers, and his eyes that see through you to your core. He wears acorns and oak leaves; oak trees have an ancient history as the most sacred of trees. He wears the sign of the moon on his head—both in its full and crescent phases. While he is primal and most ancient, there is one even more ancient: the all-mother who gave him birth. Before him stands a young maiden, ready to give herself to him. She is unafraid and defiant; just let anyone try to stop her.

Oracle Message

It might seem like a bad choice. Normally, you'd think, "No, no, I shouldn't." But right now, apparently, yes, you should. This is the card of the lord of wild things. Wildness is called for. Let yourself go. Indulge. Enjoy. Celebrate. As you do so, be aware of and honor the spiritual connection that such a practice brings. Invite nature and spirit into your soul to nurture your spirit through the delights of your senses. (Author's note: please be aware that there is decadent, wild enjoyment of the physical, and there is stupid. Don't be stupid.)

Indulge

If an opportunity for a wild things experience isn't readily available, create your own. This ritual can be used to awaken deep, perhaps forgotten, parts of your soul, feed your spirit, and inspire your mind.

Perform this exercise during the new moon. Total darkness brings its own magic. You will need to gather items that particularly indulge your senses:

- Something to eat or drink (for example, chocolate, wine, tea)
- Something to touch (a stone, a piece of fabric, a sculpture)
- Something to listen to (music, a fountain, chimes)
- Something to smell (incense, essential oils, a fire if a fireplace is available)
- Something to look at (a piece of art, a photo)

You will want a room where you will have privacy and not be disturbed. As you indulge each of your senses, seek out a corresponding reaction in your spirit. For example, some red wine may inspire you to express your passion. The heft and smoothness of a stone in your hand may speak to you of connecting and grounding with the earth. A particular incense may encourage you to seek a closer connection with the divine. In your journal, explore these connections. In the future, whenever that part of your soul needs attention, you can stimulate it by activating the corresponding sense.

CRIMSON MOON

Crimson—a color of passion, of danger, of blood. A crimson moon cannot be a pleasant omen. And yet it is the color of courage and the mother goddess.

We all live through dark, desolate times. Life, even one filled with magic, has ups and downs. Dark times have phases, just like the moon, just like all of life. Sometimes we are in shock over a new pain or loss that is fresh and sharp. Sometimes we are in the midst of mourning, where everything is as dark and black and devoid of hope as it is possible to be. And sometimes we are near the end of a dark time. The pain is not as sharp. The blackness is not as bleak. Instead, the pain is becoming part of us, not intense and cutting. It is not destroying us, but instead it is shaping who we are becoming. The darkness still hides a great deal, but it is lifting, allowing glimmers of hope to catch our eyes. We may still feel alone and a long way from happiness, but we do sense that life will continue and that maybe, just maybe, joy will be possible.

Our Crimson Moon fairy embodies this moment of darkness giving way to dawn. She stands on a pillar, disconnected still from everyday life, but she is starting to look around and see that life continues. Above her shines a slim crescent moon tinged with crimson. While much of her heart remains dark, light is beginning to show, bringing with it the courage and passion needed to deal with her loss. Behind, as yet out of sight but ready to be noticed, is a white flower, representing new growth and hope. She wears jewels of deepest red, as if made from her heart's very blood that fed her mourning. From this journey through darkness, she has grown, and these jewels represent those changes. She carries a wand that symbolizes her intent and focus. Even though she still holds it listlessly, it is starting to glow. She is beginning to feel the need to do something, that her time of weeping is almost over.

Oracle Message

Whatever you've been through, however much it has hurt, no matter how long and dark this time of loss and pain has been, you can know that it is nearly over. You are coming to terms with what has happened. It no longer cuts you harshly to think of it. You've taken that pain into your soul, and you've grown from it. You are starting to find the courage to go on. You are feeling the stirrings of the passion for life. You need only to look, and you will see the gift of hope that the universe is offering you. Then you will be ready to start a renewed phase in your life.

Charm of Hope

Even while you are going through these dark times and even as you speak of not being part of life, you still do go through the motions. Few of us are without any obligations and have the luxury of indulging our mourning. Sometimes it seems you can't possibly find the strength to get through another day, another task, another responsibility.

But get through you must. Fortunately, you can draw on the strength of the mother goddess, the universe, or whatever deity you honor to help you through. If you are having a particularly difficult time, consider enchanting your fairy charm to wear or carry with you to help you be open to the strength, courage, and hope available.

As always, you can do this enchantment whenever needed, but it is particularly powerful when done on a Tuesday, the day of Mars, suitable for courage and strength. Incorporating the power of a full or waxing moon can also boost the effectiveness.

Lay out a red cloth. Mix a few drops of clove and lavender essential oils together. If you can, place a white flower in a small vase or cup, and set it on the cloth. Anoint a red and a white candle with the oil, and light the candles, setting the red on the left and the white on the right. Lay your charm between the candles. Say three times:

> *Mother Goddess, on thee I call*
> *The days are hard; the days are long*
> *Please help me through, don't let me fall*
> *Your strength and hope shall be my song.*

If appropriate and safe, leave the charm between the candles and let them burn out. If not, snuff the candles. Wear or carry the enchanted charm to help you get through the days when you'd rather stay alone with your sadness.

Dark Enchantment

Have you ever unknowingly taken a wrong turn? How long did it take before you realized it was wrong? What clued you in? Did you deny the realization and keep going, hoping you didn't make a mistake?

Going the wrong way can lead, sometimes, to charming adventures or marvelous discoveries. More often, though, losing your way has negative effects. Minimally, it is lost time. Worse, it can mean a missed event or flight. Worse still, it can lead to dangerous areas. Even though we mostly believe in free will and that our paths are not pre-destined, we usually have a sense of feeling like we're on the right track, that we're doing exactly what we should be doing and moving in the direction we want to go. And sometimes we feel like we're on the wrong track. Sometimes we know exactly where that wrong choice occurred, and sometimes we have no idea how it happened. But what if it did happen and now we're where we never intended to go? What can we do then?

A lovely, ethereal fairy, pale as moonlight and dark as a mystery, looks at you. You can't tell, but it seems as if she smiles and there is mischief in her eyes. But you look again, and it's the oddest thing—suddenly she has no expression at all. She is adorned with lush leaves and elegant tattoos of spirals and the moon. She carries a black candle, as if promising protection from the dark. And a moth is, naturally enough, drawn to her flame. Everything seems okay; good, even. Candle, leaves, spirals, moons. She can't be bad, right? You find yourself drawn to her like—well, like a moth to a flame. And we all know what happened to that moth.

Oracle Message

You want to go somewhere or do something. You have convinced yourself that all is well. This choice will definitely further your goals and take you in the direction you wish to go. At the very most, you think it won't lead you too far astray. You say there is nothing overtly wrong with what you are considering. Besides, you really, really want to. Take a hint from the late moth: don't go there. Whatever it is, however tempting, it is not going to be good for you in the long run. Whatever it is may seem small, but this is no normal little temptation. This has the potential to take you off your course and in a direction you really don't want to go.

Eyes on the Prize

Whatever your goals—short-term, long-term, huge, or small—sometimes you need help staying motivated. Other possibilities weave their dark enchantments, and let's face it: sometimes we'd like to veer off-course and not worry about getting back. The following spell can help you stay focused.

Write your goal on a piece of paper, fold it up, and place a carnelian or rose quartz on it. Set a gold or orange candle nearby. Every morning when you get up, light the candle, unfold the paper, and read it out loud. Fold up the paper, and set it back down. Hold the carnelian or rose quartz in your dominant hand. Gaze into the flame, and say three times:

I know where I am going
I know exactly what I want
With every step I am showing
I know exactly what I want.

If a mirror is nearby, look at your reflection and smile. There's a woman who won't be lured from her path. Snuff out the candle and replace the carnelian or rose quartz. Repeat every day for as long as is necessary.

DARK QUEEN

Are you ready to walk through the door? Ready to lift the veil? What door, what veil? Ah, that which separates the sacred from the mundane, that which separates the answers from the questions.

Undoubtedly there are times when we would love to see the bigger picture. We can usually trust that things are happening as they should, that we are on the right path, that there is a lesson or blessing in loss if only we could see it. But sometimes we feel like children who are told, "You'll understand when you're older"—like we'll get the lesson or see the blessing "someday," when we've somehow "earned that right." But can't we know now? Isn't there some way to penetrate the threshold between the mundane and the spiritual worlds? Can't we understand the mysteries? Why can't we just know that answer or the reason? There must be a way.

One glance at the Dark Queen and you know she'll tell you, and in no uncertain terms. And she'll let you know that you probably aren't ready. Clad in black and red, she's ready to protect the sacred mysteries of the universe. Her staff, representing her wisdom and her will, is tall and slender, an elegant weapon. And she wields it with grace and speed. However, she does, on occasion, impart some wisdom. Surrounding her are eight ravens, ready to do her bidding. If someone worthy and in dire need asks with all sincerity, she will send an answer, even if the seeker isn't ready.

Oracle Message

The good news is that the answer and understanding you seek can be found. The bad news is that you want to understand something that may be best left a mystery. Consider letting it go. If you persist, your prayers will be heard, and you will find the answer. As befits a gift from the Dark Queen, it will be like a double-edged sword: it will cut through your confusion, but it will also hurt. As also befits the Dark Queen's nature, the answer will be veiled and hidden. You will have to find it. Be alert for signs; seek in the quiet corners of your soul. Or maybe you'll change your mind and be content not to know.

If You Must

If you are looking for an answer to a mystery and you are determined to get it, you might try going straight to the Dark Queen herself.

In a quiet room where you won't be disturbed, light frankincense and a white candle. Sit in a chair with your feet on the ground or lie down if you prefer.

Look at the Dark Queen card and memorize it. When you're ready, close your eyes.

See yourself walking toward her. Feel the chill air and the slight breeze as the ravens fly and swoop around you. Hear the squawking and calls of the ravens. Feel a feather gently brush your cheek. See the otherworldly glow radiating from the door behind her.

You can't help but feel her power; her presence deters most from approaching the door. Try not to stare at her staff. Probably she won't use it on you.

Introduce yourself.

From here on out, you're on your own.

DRAGON WITCH

Have you ever wished you had an extra reserve of energy that you could tap into? Sometimes you want just an extra little boost. You have a feeling it is there, if only you knew the secret that would allow you to access it.

The world is filled with different types of energy that are appropriate for different purposes. This elemental energy is often seen as earth, air, fire, and water. Each type has its own properties. Earth energy is grounded and practical, useful for manifesting tangible goals. Air energy promotes clarity of thought and problem solving. Water provides emotional richness and creativity. Fire energy is all about drive and passion. There are lots of practices that allow you to access, focus, and use these energies. One way is to visualize them as creatures that embody certain characteristics, such as a sylph or bird for air or a sprite or mermaid for water. Dragons are ideal representations for fire energy and are also traditional symbols of personal power. If you want to incorporate drive and passion into your life, exploring dragon magic is an ideal practice.

The Dragon Witch is a keeper of dragons. She can handle and direct them, though no one can really tame them. She is an expert in the properties and use of fire energy. Behind her is a Celtic knot interwoven with a pentacle. This represents the complex interconnection of all things with the elemental energies of the universe, including spirit. She wears a crescent moon headpiece with three jewels, acknowledging her devotion to the goddess. The three jewels represent the triple goddess, but the main symbol is the crescent. This is appropriate, because fire energy is never stable, always waxing or waning. She also wears a cross, a union of the world of spirit and the physical world. Her expertise and power come from a well-balanced understanding of both realms. In her hand she holds a small dragon, representing her area of expertise. Naturally, she wears red, the color of fire, passion, and energy.

Oracle Message

Whatever it is you wish to accomplish, you are very close to doing so, but your energy or drive may be waning. Now is the time to give yourself a burst of energy so you can successfully complete your task. Take a deep breath, focus your mind, set your intent, and finish what you've started. Victory is at hand, but you have a little way to go before it is complete. The power you need is within your reach. Connect with your inner dragon, and you won't be disappointed.

Get Fired Up

You're near the end of an arduous task, or perhaps you are just beginning an ambitious project. You'll want all the energy you can muster. You'll need to find your inner dragon. Mix together a little clove, cinnamon, neroli, and bergamot essential oils. This is a spicy, fiery blend, so use it carefully.

Anoint a red candle with the oil, and light it. In a quiet room where you won't be disturbed, sit comfortably with your feet on the ground or lie down if you prefer. Imagine a landscape with jagged mountains and deep caves. See yourself exploring and climbing, searching for your dragon. Once you find it, examine it closely.

Note its color, its wings, all of its unique features. Watch it (from a safe distance, obviously) as it breathes its fiery breath. That expression of power is awesome, isn't it? Watch as its strong wings lift its weight, and see its elegant movement through the sky. Recognize that this is a symbol of your inner fire, your power and drive. It is there for you to use when you need it.

DRAGONESS

Are you the hunter or the hunted, the predator or the prey? Thankfully, in our day-to-day lives, we are mostly neither. Or are we? In how many small ways do we exhibit these tendencies? Maybe some of us are exhilarated by the thrill of the hunt. Maybe some of us feel fated to be hunted.

Being a predator involves seeking out and taking from others. This could take the form of belittling someone; that is, taking some of their self-esteem to build up your own. Or it could be cutting someone off in traffic, invading their space and safety to advance your own journey. It could be something more, such as deceiving someone;

61

this ultimately takes away their faith in you, in their own judgment, and in others. That's a lot to take away from someone. Or you could be the prey. You could be the one belittled, cut off, deceived. How do you recover? How do you guard against it in the future? Can you guard against it? Is there ever an appropriate time to willfully play one role or the other?

This Dragoness is, by her nature, a predator. As is clear by her wings, she is a fairy descended from dragon lineage. She inherited not only the wing structure of her dragon ancestors but also their characteristics: powerful, protective, and acquisitive. She is clothed in purple, with wings of deep purple, which is associated with the power of the ancients, such as dragons. She sits on a high pillar, so that she may watch over and protect her territory. Here, she is shown with three crescent moons. They are all waiting to be filled and represent her longing that is never completely satisfied.

Oracle Message

Either you or someone you are inquiring about is currently in the role of predator. Are you seeking to take something from someone else? Trying to get ahead at someone else's expense? Building up your own image while tearing down another's? Or is there someone near you who is taking from you, perhaps so subtly that you don't even know it? Examine your actions and your relationships. Are you the hunter or the hunted? And are you okay with that? Whether you are the predator or the prey, this card suggests that you carefully consider your behavior before you continue.

Sometimes You Need to Be the Dragon

It is not often when it is appropriate to act like a dragon. But there are times when someone else is sapping your energy and messing in your life, and some protective, powerful action must be taken. When you need to feel powerful and need to protect yourself or your loved ones, perform the visualization and charm enchantment below. You can do this anytime it is needed, but it is particularly powerful if done during the full moon, and avoid a waning moon if you can, as a waning moon represents a diminishing of power.

Power Visualization

Sit comfortably with your feet on the ground (or lie down if you prefer) where you won't be disturbed or interrupted. Visualize yourself standing on a pillar, perhaps like the one the Dragoness crouches on. Stand tall and confidently. Imagine small dots of all colors surrounding you in a large circle, representing the positive strength and power of the universe. Raise your arms out to shoulder height, and see the colors burst forth in great beams of light, sparkling vividly. Raise your arms straight up, and see the colors swirl and swirl until they gather above your head and pour down through your fingertips, filling you with the positive power and strength of the universe.

As you go through your day and feel the need for power, just wiggle your fingertips (discreetly), and you'll remember the feeling of all those colors and all that power filling you.

Power Charm Enchantment

Lay out a black cloth. On it, place a small glass of water, a bit of soil or salt, a lit purple candle, and a feather. Anoint your fairy charm and a bit of obsidian with some clove oil, and place them on the cloth. Say three times:

> *By water, fire, earth, and air*
> *And powers of the spirit realm*
> *Empower this gem and charm*
> *Allow my power to shine fair.*
> *So let it be.*

Snuff out the candle. Wear your enchanted fairy charm and carry the obsidian as a reminder of your power.

EMERALD PRINCESS

Even the shyest and quietest among us have, at times, felt a deep stirring in our souls to speak out, to rock the boat, to create a ruckus, to try to change something.

There are times when someone, some rule, or some policy doesn't seem right or fair. It may be a minor irritation, like someone telling you that you "cannot bring that beverage in here." Or it could be a larger issue, like a rule that unfairly hurts someone. Some rules may be irritating or annoying, but they serve a purpose and are really not worth flouting. But then there are those situations that demand your attention: an animal being mistreated, a rule that is unfair, someone being hurt. Even though it may be easier to ignore the situation, something inside you urges you on. You find within yourself the bravery needed to fight for the cause.

The Emerald Princess seems almost invisible. Blending in to her environment so perfectly, she nearly disappears. Her long, black tresses swirl and mingle with the seaweed that adorns her watery world. She is wrapped in a long cord beaded with jewels, each jewel a bit of wisdom. She is posed near a crescent shape, which reminds us that, like the moon during that phase, she is mostly hidden. She just stays quietly, moving gently with the flow, silently observing and gathering bits of wisdom for her cord. But when it is necessary, she stirs. Water, her natural environment, often represents the soul. When she stirs, something similar stirs in us, in our soul. It wakens us to the need for defiance. Yes, this nearly invisible, quiet little beauty has the power to start revolutions.

Oracle Message

There is something going on that doesn't seem right to you. You are feeling, perhaps uncharacteristically, the need to flout authority, to raise your voice, to stand up for yourself or someone else. Check that impulse. If it is something that is fundamentally immature or reckless, consider letting it slide. However, and probably more likely, if it is something more, now is the time to be bold and speak up. If your moral, spiritual, or ethical beliefs compel you to defy something and you don't, you may regret it later. And who knows? Your boldness could very well spark beneficial change in your life or even in the world.

ENTWINED

Romantic love provides life with some of the highest highs and lowest lows people ever experience. No wonder it is the focus of so many readings. When enjoying the first blush of romantic love, two people often feel entwined, like they've found a missing part of their soul. It's a time filled with exhilaration, strength, and vulnerability.

While there is quite a bit going on inside, the outside world almost entirely ceases to exist for those in the midst of new love. The focus is on the other. And why not? There is a new person to discover and complex, exciting emotions to explore. While you may feel you've known the other person for lifetimes, there is still a sense of the unknown. Also, you are discovering the person you become in this person's presence. No wonder there is little time or desire for mundane, day-to-day living.

Besides the wonders of love, there is some possibility of danger here. Being caught up in the feeling of being in love can blind you to things that would normally catch your attention and perhaps raise red flags. Also, focusing solely on a new relationship can damage other aspects of your life. Becoming out of balance is a very real danger.

In this card, a male and female mermaid drift together in a tender embrace. Seaweed swirls around them, as if to bind their souls together for eternity. Behind them, the moon shines a gentle silvery light that highlights their best features and quietly masks their flaws. Their eyes are closed while their heads touch. While they are certainly thinking of each other, they are not necessarily looking at each other. They are seeing, in their mind's eye, the very best version of the other person. She holds a luminous pearl, an echo of the moon. While the moon's light beautifully highlights and hides reality, so our entwined mermaids do the same for each.

Oracle Message

Romantic love is clearly the focus here. This experience is one of the most exciting and fulfilling that many people have. It is often short-lived, so do enjoy it as much as you can. Do not worry when the energy of it lessens, as this is natural. Do be aware that as it does, you both will start seeing each other with your eyes open and in the bright light of the sun, not the forgiving light of the moon. Love, just like the moon, has phases, and each one is its own adventure. If you are seeking to fall in love, this card is a positive omen.

Call a Little Love

This is a very simple spell to help draw love into your life. This spell is best done any time but a waning moon. Use a small pink candle. Carve a heart shape into it, and anoint it with rose essential oil. Set it before a mirror and light it. If possible, put your fairy charm on a pink or red ribbon, anoint it with rose oil, and lay it near the candle. Gaze into the flame, and say three times:

> *Brilliant moon shining in the dark*
> *My heart does call, my heart does yearn.*
> *Hear my prayer and let love spark.*
> *Send love to me, let passion burn.*
> *So let it be.*

If appropriate and safe, let the candle burn itself out. If that is not possible, snuff out the flame. Wear or carry the fairy charm.

Torn Between Two Lovers?

If you are attracted to two possible lovers and don't know which is your best choice, use your fairy charm as a pendulum to help you decide. Use a piece of pink paper or use pink or red ink on white paper. Write one lover's name horizontally and one vertically with a cross in the middle, like this:

LOVER 1

LOVER 2

Hold the pendulum so that it hangs in the center of the heart you drew. Quiet your mind. Ask the universe to let you know which is the best choice for you at this time. If the pendulum moves horizontally, it is the first name; if vertically, it is the second name. If it doesn't move or goes in a circle, then neither is right for you at this time.

GOTHIC ROSE

Throughout our lives we play many roles. Sometimes there are rituals that mark our change from one to another, like graduation or marriage. Mostly, though, our changes go unmarked. But they still happen.

Changes and transformations take place on many levels, some obvious and external, like starting a new job. Some are more internal, like shifts in our spiritual or psychological views. Sometimes these personal transformations coincide with a dark time in our lives. The dark time may be in response to a loss of some sort. It could just as easily be a conscious withdrawing, kind of like putting yourself into a cocoon. It is an odd and intriguing mystery how so many miraculous changes take place in the dark, unseen by anyone, sometimes unseen even by the person experiencing them. And, even with consciously initiated transformation, you cannot always be sure what the final outcome will be.

The Gothic Rose sorceress knows all about transformations. She abides amongst black roses, symbols of the exquisite beauty of the mysterious growth that occurs in the darkest, most secret places. She holds a black orb, a seed of nothing and of everything. In it are all possibilities. Not until it has sprouted, grown, and bloomed will she know for certain what it will be. Her gloves are adorned with a slim crescent moon, because even though her arms plant the seeds, the outcome is still hidden. Her eyes have endless tears because she never forgets that during the miracle of new life, old life must be sacrificed. And so she mourns the loss of all life even as she creates new life. Above her is a stunning moth, a clear sign of the completed transformative process. As the moth emerges from the dark and closed cocoon, it spreads its wings and flies toward the light.

Oracle Message

You are in some phase of transformation. This can be a scary and exciting time. You may not even know what is coming next, but you'll be eager to find out. Spend time getting to know the new you. How are you different? How are you the same? What effect will these changes have on your life? What excites you the most? What frightens you or makes you nervous? One of the dangers of this period is the desire to stay within your metaphorical cocoon. It is, after all, a safe place. And who knows what life as the new you is going to be like. There is always a bit of stress with anything new. That's all natural, but don't let it stop you. Like the Gothic Rose's moth, reveal your beautiful, new self, and fly toward the light!

Time to Change

Transformations can happen without you knowing it. Or you can decide you want to re-create some aspect of yourself. Transformations don't happen overnight, so there is no quick spell that you can do tonight to wake up tomorrow as a different person. But you can focus your intent and help the magical process along. Before you begin, make sure you are clear about how you'd like to change.

Work this enchantment during the new moon, if possible. Mix together sandalwood and rose essential oils. Place the container with the mixed oil in front of a purple candle. Place a moonstone or quartz crystal in front of the container of blended oils. Light the candle, and say three times:

All life changes
All life grows
Time to rearrange
And let it show.
Goddess, guide me
Help me through
I am very eager to see
The me that's new.

If appropriate and safe, let the candle burn out. If not, snuff out the candle. Apply a drop of the enchanted oil to your wrists and the middle of your forehead. Repeat daily as needed.

GOTHIQUE

What scares you? What do you do when you're afraid? Is fear a good thing that helps keep you from danger, or is it a roadblock?

Fear takes many forms. It is a basic instinct. We may be afraid of walking down a dark street alone, for example. That sort of fear is meant to keep us safe; who knows what is lurking there? Other fears arise from experience: you use a hot pad to take a pan from the oven for fear of burning your hand. Some of these fears can be beneficial as well. Sometimes, though, we generalize one experience, and it keeps us from trying again. You approach someone at a party, and they brush you off. The rejection and

83

embarrassment stick with you, and you avoid that again for fear of having the same experience. Some fears, like the fear of speaking in public, develop in your mind because you worry that something bad will happen. Fear can keep you safe. It can also keep you from moving forward with your life. The key with any particular fear is to determine if you should honor it or overcome it.

The Gothique fairy represents fears that can be conquered. Behind her is a full moon shrouded with purple clouds, representing the reward for those who face her. Purple is a color of spirituality and personal power. The full moon is the moon in her whole glory, where all of her knowledge and influence is revealed. Before you experience your own power, knowledge, and ability, though, you must face Gothique. She stands before you, her eyes daring you to pass her. She wears a small headpiece with a single purple jewel. Her one intent is to test your personal power. She holds a tall staff crowned with a black crescent moon and purple ribbon. This is her weapon—the dark crescent is wisdom hidden by irrationality, the purple ribbon is your power bound to her will. To pass her, you must seek understanding and banish irrationality as well as reclaim your own power.

Oracle Message

There is something you fear. Wherever that fear came from, however it entered your mind, however well it may have served you in the past, it is now keeping you from moving forward. If you do not face it, you are frozen in place. If you do face it, you will not only continue along your chosen path but you will also gain strength and understanding beyond your expectations.

Fear Itself

You've come to a roadblock. You know what is stopping you. You know that this is a fear to conquer, not honor. But how? These journaling questions can help you devise a plan of action.

1. Identify your fear. Write out exactly what it is you are afraid of, in as much detail as possible.

2. Is this fear based on past experience? If so, how is it similar? How is it different? Do the similarities clearly indicate the same outcome as your past experience? Do the differences hint at ways the outcome may be different?

3. How many different outcomes can you imagine? Write them all out. What is the key difference that changes the outcomes in each scenario? In the best-case scenario, is the key something you

can control? What would your life be like if that best-case scenario occurred? In the worst-case scenario, what is the outcome? What would your life be like if that happened? Imagine how you could use that experience in a positive way.

4. Think of a person you admire and who you think could overcome this fear. Imagine how she would approach it. Write down what you think her plan would be. How can you make that plan your own?

5. Imagine a friend is in the same situation and she came to you for advice. What would you tell her? How would you help her overcome her fear?

Green Man

So often, magical workings and oracle messages are about claiming your power, controlling your own life, and seeking what you want. But what kind of magic and power can be found in sacrifice?

As with so many things, sacrifice can be a positive or negative choice. At its worst, it is pointless martyrdom for the sake of attention or melodrama. Certainly you've seen this sort of behavior and perhaps even indulged in it yourself. At its best, it is a quiet, selfless act that deeply blesses someone else's life. Sacrifices take many shapes and come in many sizes. Giving up a seat on a crowded bus is a small act, but you may never know what positive consequences could come of it. Whether the sacrifice is big or small, spontaneous or elaborately planned, the effects can be magical. Often the person making the sacrifice experiences a sense of fulfillment and joy. Even more interesting, such an action can inspire an unexpected feeling of humbleness and gratitude for being allowed to be a part of such a beautiful story. Much of magic is about understanding the flow of the universe and working with it to achieve your goals. How much more powerful, then, is the magic of working with the universe to achieve *its* goals?

The Green Man is an interesting character with Celtic origins. He represents the masculine energies associated with nature, most commonly trees and plants. In some festivals, an effigy of the Green Man is dunked in a river or lake to guarantee enough rain for the season's crops. In the autumn, he is ritually sacrificed and reborn in the spring. Just as nature has many cycles and phases, so does the Green Man. Here, we see the autumnal Green Man, with leaves starting to change. His eyes are sad, as if he is fully aware that a hard task awaits him. The time is nearing for him to make the ultimate sacrifice, to give his life. In an act that seems so vulnerable, so passive, he creates his most powerful magic. He provides the promise and spark for new life.

Oracle Message

You are being asked to make a sacrifice. You need to give up something. Probably you don't want to; that's why it's a sacrifice. It may not be easy and it may not be fun. But in the long run, you will be glad you did. This will be an unexpectedly powerful experience, one that you couldn't imagine. Beyond the good feeling of helping someone, you'll find humility and honor at being given this opportunity. Through it, you will develop a better understanding of and closer relationship with the universe, the goddess, or whatever deity you honor.

The Gift of Giving

When you give up something, probably you'd like to be thanked for it. In this case, you may or may not be. Whether you are or not, you might want to thank the universe for this opportunity to serve and to be part of the greater good. Use this simple little prayer to do just that.

Carve an image of a leaf on a green candle (or cut out the shape of a leaf from green paper and place it under the candle holder). Anoint the candle with oakmoss oil or burn oakmoss incense. Green is the color of the Green Man, and the leaf is his symbol. Oakmoss is a scent associated with earthiness and gratitude. Say the following as many times as you wish, until you feel your gratitude has been expressed:

Thanks be to thee
Green Man of Life
For your gift to me.
You gave the seed
To let me ease
Someone's need.
Thanks be to thee
For your gift to me.

When you are finished, snuff out the candle.

Green Woman

There are times when we need direction—when we aren't sure what to do. But sometimes we know exactly what we want to do and are focused on making that happen.

Just as there are different phases of the moon that are appropriate for different endeavors, there are different elemental energies available to you. Fire is about passion and drive. Water deals with emotions and creativity. Air aids in thought processes and problem solving. Earth is the practical element; it manifests things. It is the element of the physical realm. The physical realm can feel mundane and perhaps not worthy of spiritual attention, but that is not so. Magic is about creating change in the world we live in, the physical world. Indeed, some see the elements as all working in a progression to make change happen. Fire provides the inspiration; water supplies the emotional commitment; air supplies the plan; and earth is the actual finishing.

The masked Green Woman understands the earth. She celebrates its power. She seeks its wisdom. She honors its cycles of life and death. By wearing this mask, she does not intend to hide something (as is often the case with masks). Rather, she wishes to see the world through the eyes of the earth. By doing so, she can further understand the connections between all living things. By the jewel set in the mask between her eyes, she can also harness, focus, and use earth energy to accomplish her goals. Behind her is a full moon, a symbol of her commitment to completing the task at hand.

Oracle Message

This message is simple: it is time to finish what you've started. Or if you haven't started it yet, what are you wait-

ing for? The project might be big. Or it could be small...
like maybe cleaning out a closet. Whatever it is that has
been on your "to do" list, now is the time to cross it off.

Roll Up Your Sleeves

Earth energy is really useful for the type of cleaning or
organizing that includes getting rid of things. Just as plants
cannot be too crowded if they are to grow strong, people
usually function better without excess clutter ("excess" is a
relative term and can vary from person to person). Cleaning
something out, clearing the space, is a magical act. It makes
room in your life for something new. So if you are feeling
in a rut or bogged down, get rid of some stuff and invite
fresh energy in. Before you begin, say four times (four is a
number of stability and is associated with the earth):

> *Out with the old, the saying goes*
> *And ends it thus: in with the new*
> *As I begin, a fresh wind blows*
> *And soon my life has a new view.*

GYPSY ROSE

Whatever our age, there are times when we feel carefree and young. And then, probably all too often, there are times when we don't.

Being carefree and young feels good. Feeling this way fills us with an enthusiasm for life. Responsibilities, obligations, "real life"—all these can dull or even quash that feeling. No wonder, since being weighted down with the cares of daily life is the opposite of being carefree. While it is neither wise nor practical to throw away all our cares and responsibilities, it is also unwise (and no fun at all) to let cares and worries erase enthusiasm and simple joy from our lives.

In Gypsy Rose, we see a lovely fairy looking back at us a bit sadly. She is about to cross a threshold to a brighter, more colorful realm. She would like us to follow, but she's getting the feeling that we won't. Clothed in white, she expresses a pure desire for all the good things the universe has to offer. Orange roses represent enthusiasm and desire. The orange jewel of her headpiece is attached with many cords, showing that she intentionally weaves enthusiasm and joy through her life. Her colorful wings take her on glorious flights of fancy. The world she is about to enter glows with light even though a crescent moon is high in the sky. Is she looking at the world through rose-colored glasses? Perhaps. Perhaps the rose-colored glasses aren't meant to change the way the world looks, but to shade out cares and worries so we can see the world at its vibrant best.

Oracle Message

Maybe you've been working too hard or worrying too much. Now is the time to take a break. Do something that makes your heart leap with excitement. It doesn't have to be a big leap. Rediscover a lost pleasure, revisit a favorite place, make plans with friend. Put away your troubles just for a little while (you can attend to them when you get back), and enjoy life. You may even find that your outlook changes, and things really aren't as bleak or hard as you thought. In the meantime, indulge and enjoy.

Playful Magic

There is no enchantment, no oils or candles, no journaling. Just this: go play!

INNOCENCE

Whether you are a mother or just have a mother, we all know that the subject of mothers is complex. But here we are looking at a specific aspect of motherhood: its relationship with providing care.

In its ideal form, the love of a mother for her child is selfless, pure, and unconditional. She is devoted to the care of her child. She will sacrifice herself for him. Her love is not marred by an agenda; it is innocent. She holds the tiny life close to her. He reaches out, forming his first relationship. And he is pure and simple. The mother and baby nurture one another, giving to each other in different ways. In life, things are less than ideal, but still, we understand that the responsibility of the care of an innocent, new life is major. It takes sacrifices, strength, and wisdom that we may not have imagined.

Motherhood, the practice of being a mother, can take many forms. We may be called to take care of something or someone that has nothing to do with babies. Caring for someone in this way can also be gift, similar to motherhood. It can be an unusually satisfying experience.

This image, of the innocent mother and baby fairies, is one of those tender, touching images that really is worth a thousand words. Mother and child cling together. Although the mother acknowledges us with a glance, we know that this attention is fleeting. In less than a moment, her focus will be back on her baby. For the time being, they are each other's whole world. Her purple gown, representing her personal power, is bound with a white ribbon, representing purity and spirituality. She is using all her abilities for one purpose only: to care for this baby.

Oracle Message

Care needs to be given, and it's up to you to give it. It may be a person or animal, an event, or a project. Whatever it is, there is a need for you to focus, at least for a while, only on it. You will need to put some of your own needs and desires on the back burner for the time being, and attend to the need at hand. This card could also mean that you are the one in need and you should accept the care and help that is being offered.

JEWEL OF THE SEA

Beauty, they say, is in the eye of the beholder. Some say otherwise, that beauty is the inner light shining out. Grace is moving through the world in beauty. Is beauty merely physical, or does it come from somewhere else? In fairy magic, there is a kind of magic called glamour. With that magic, fairies can make themselves appear more beautiful. That magic is available to those who seek it.

Who hasn't wished she were more physically beautiful? We all have beauty within us, but how do we make that beauty shine through? If we feel beautiful, we usually are more confident and less self-conscious. By expressing our inner beauty, we can move with grace through our lives, enchanting them and touching the lives of others with magic. We can be more beautiful by expressing that which is good, compassionate, wise, and generous within ourselves. Ah, but first, we must acknowledge that this beauty does indeed dwell in our souls.

In this card, we see a charming Jewel of the Sea. Although she is still at this moment, it doesn't take much to imagine her moving with grace and beauty through her world. Her flowing white hair indicates purity of thought and intention. She is crowned with treasures from the sea floor, showing deep, ancient wisdom. A shining bubble surrounds her head. It is the certain knowledge and belief that she is truly beautiful. She radiates light, even in the darkest depths of the ocean. A point of light adorns her fingertip, and she knows she can spread beauty and light with the wave of her hand. She leaves bits of sparkly magic behind wherever she goes.

Oracle Message

Acknowledge your beauty. Recognize it, nurture it, honor it. Realize where your beauty comes from. Look at all that is good and wise within you. Commit to cultivating it. Be secure in your beauty and make good use of it. Let your every action, thought, and word be an extension and expression of your inner beauty. Leave beauty and magic behind you wherever you go. Recognize and honor the beauty in others.

A Little Glamour Never Hurt

Cultivating inner beauty is all very well and good. But sometimes a girl just wants to feel, you know, *beautiful*. Here's a simple little spell that might provide just the pick-me-up you're looking for.

Mix a few drops of rose and sandalwood essential oils. Draw a warm, comfortable bath. Light a grey candle (grey is useful in glamour spells). Add some of the rose and sandalwood oil to the bath. Relax in the lightly scented, warm water. Lean back. Close your eyes. Visualize yourself at your best. Notice all your beautiful parts and imagine how you will dress to accentuate them. See yourself moving through the day (or evening) with beauty and grace. See the smiles, feel the magic.

When you are done and ready to dress, wear lavender-colored undies. I know, I know. But lavender is a color of personal power, spirituality, and fairy magic. Just try it.

Don't forget to snuff out the candle.

Cast a Spell on Yourself

Many people spend time and energy reminding themselves how they fall short of perfection. Here's a different approach. For thirty days, commit to reminding yourself at least once a day of your beautiful qualities. Pick three to five things about yourself that you like. Each day, look in the mirror and remind yourself of your amazing qualities. Be as bold and enthusiastic with your praise as you usually are with your criticism.

"Look at those eyes! They're freakin' *gorgeous*!"

"Ohmygawd! Check out that hair: *fabulous.*"

"On me, this outfit *totally* rocks."

Be careful, being nice to yourself is addictive, and worse, can lead to excessive niceness to others.

LAVENDER MOON

It's hard to journey through life without learning quite a bit. Facts and such are one thing. But spiritual truths, life philosophies, general ethics—well, they are another.

By nature, seekers search for answers and truth. We seek a closer relationship with the divine. We are always looking for something. There does come a point, though, when we have so much information—we have read so many books and heard so many opinions—that we have to turn away from more knowledge and sift through what we've gathered. Away from the opinions and judgments of others, in a place where we feel safe and at ease, we need to examine each idea, belief, and practice and measure it against our own soul. Those that resonate and feel right we keep and synthesize into our belief system. Those that do not we respectfully put away from us. Not everything is for everybody. We all have our own unique path. It is up to us to find it.

The Lavender Moon fairy is doing her own seeking. Surrounded by shades of purple, she is prepared for spiritual work. She incorporates the power of the full moon because she desires illumination. She wants her path to be revealed. The moths around her symbolize transformation and a desire for light. She herself is going through a transformation, and her final step is deciding her path, determining what is right for her. She calmly and reverently asks for guidance as she begins her inward journey.

Oracle Message

It is time for you to be very clear with yourself about what you believe. This may pertain to a spiritual path decision. Or it may pertain to a smaller issue. Whichever it is, you have all the information you need. It is time to stop researching, reading, and asking others. Take all the information you have gathered, and withdraw. Be alone with these ideas, and measure them against nothing but your own heart. Only then will you know what is right for you.

Sacred Space

When you withdraw to consider your path, you may find it useful to create a sacred space. Work in a room where you will not be disturbed. First, cleanse the room by smudging it with sage. To promote balance, make a small altar. Lay a purple or white cloth on a flat surface. On it, place a small glass or bowl of water, a white or purple candle, a small amount of earth or salt or a quartz crystal, and lavender incense. Light the candle and the incense. Say:

By water, fire, earth, and air
Let the space so sacred be
Keep it safe and keep it clear
Just for me. So let it be.

When you are ready to get started, you can sit in a chair, sit cross-legged on the floor, lie down, or sit at a desk if you plan to journal. After you are done, snuff the candle and incense, and put your things away. If you come back to finish (you may not finish in one sitting), you probably don't need to re-smudge, but set out your altar, light the candle and incense, repeat the enchantment, and begin. Repeat as needed.

Direct Line to the Divine

There may be times when you are too confused, too tired, or too invested in a situation and just know that you can't make an objective decision. In times like these, a little divine direction can come in very handy. If you have several options and you're not sure which is the best for you, draw a circle and bisect it with lines labeled with your choice, like so:

Using your fairy charm as a pendulum, hold it over the center of the circle, and say, "Fairy, fairy, show the way; what's the best path for me today?" Repeat and focus your intent until your pendulum indicates your best option for the day.

LOVE SPRINGS ETERNAL

The foundation of a solid relationship is one of the joys of a happy life. In the beginning of love, lovers see the best, unflawed version of each other. They are focused on the intense emotion and exhilaration of being in love. As love matures, lovers see each other with their eyes open. They see the other's strengths and weaknesses. They let each other's strengths shine and grow; they provide help and guidance in areas of weakness. They stand in amazement to see how they really do fit together.

While in romantic love, we are sometimes worried about it ending, about falling out of love, about becoming bored. As true love grows, it becomes more confident. Through the ups and downs of daily life, love becomes familiar and dependable, giving us strength. And as time goes by, it never loses its luster. You get a twinkle in your eye as a smile is shared; your heart jumps when you catch an unexpected glimpse of your lover; a scent in the air brings back a memory, and your insides turn to jelly.

Two fairies stand confidently before each other, holding each other, as if promising eternal support. The sun shines on them, illuminating their world and each other. They can see each other clearly; nothing is hidden. Even knowing the other's weaknesses or faults, they love each other more than ever. They stand on a bridge, showing how their relationship has joined two lives. The trees behind them form a heart, surrounding them in a deeply rooted love. The white flowers show the purity of their love that has stood the test of time. The glittering jewels on her dress represent the sparkle of passion that binds ⸱m still.

Oracle Message

This love can only be the result of time. This is a love with roots that go deeply into the earth and branches that reach toward the sun, always seeking truth and opportunities to grow. This is a love that focuses on being the best partner you can—that allows you to be the best you can be and provides a safe place for you to grow. Is that where you are at? Is it where you want to be? If you are in a relationship that isn't quite there yet, this card indicates that it is possible, but it may need a little attention and nurturing.

To Make Love Strong

Such a love as this card represents does not just happen. Those who are given it are entrusted to take care of it. If you are in such a relationship or think your relationship can become this, this spell, along with the journaling exercises, will help your love grow strong and truly spring eternal.

Plant a lavender or rosemary plant in a pot with a small bit of rose quartz buried in the soil. Keep the plant in a sunny window somewhere where you can see it as you write in your journal. Each time you write in your journal, use the following questions to guide your writing. You may wish to spend more than one entry on each subject.

1. What would happen to your plant if it got too much or too little water? Symbolically, water often represents emotions. How is your relationship affected if you react quickly, based on emotion, without thinking things through? How is your relationship affected if you withhold your emotions and don't share what you are feeling? How do you feel when your partner lashes out emotionally, or withholds or withdraws? In the natural world, there are times of drought and of too much rain. In any relationship, there will be an ebb and flow of emotional give and take. Do you have healthy, effective ways to cope during these times?

122

2. What would happen if your plant received too much or not enough sunlight? Symbolically, light often represents thought processes or thinking. How is your relationship affected if you think too much about something, worry excessively, or obsess about something? Conversely, what is the effect if you are thoughtless and don't consider how your actions affect your partner?

3. Houseplants can do lots on their own. They can turn sunlight into food for themselves. They can turn carbon dioxide into oxygen. Yet they cannot get their own water; they cannot put themselves in a sunny window. Your partner can do lots of things. What are some things they cannot do or that you do better? How can you help them be and feel like a stronger person? In what ways would you like to be helped or supported? In what ways do you make a perfect team? In what ways are you not so perfect?

MAIDEN MOON

Timing, as they say, is everything. We pay attention to time in so many ways. We acknowledge the importance of large chunks of time, such as childhood or summertime. We celebrate birthdays and other annual events. We mark the passing of days and months with a calendar. Some of us organize our time down to the hour with a daily planner.

Then there is another, more nebulous concept of time. If we have something to tell someone, we may "wait until the time is right," even if we don't know exactly when that will be. Sometimes we may break off a relationship or refuse a project, saying, "This just isn't a good time."

These sorts of times aren't measured by a clock or a calendar. They are spaces in time created by circumstance.

The moon has her own timing and phases. Each phase has different energy and can be used to enhance the magic in your own life. Below is a brief idea of what each phase is particularly suited for.

New moon: beginnings

Waxing: growing and increasing

Full: completion, the full power of the moon

Waning: decreasing, eliminating, banishing

So, for example, if you wanted to start a new diet, setting a starting date during a waning or new moon would be better than during a waxing moon.

Experienced practitioners of moon magic break the phases down even further. They also pay attention to what astrological sign the moon is in, as those positions bring their own specific energies.

126

Our Maiden Moon is a priestess dedicated to honoring the moon. She holds a wand topped with a full white moon, to gather and focus the moon's power. She wears a slim black crescent about her waist, because every phase of the moon should be respected. The hem of her gown is decorated with spirals and swirls to remind her that all her magic affects the flow of the universe. Her calla lilies are signs of grace and beauty, the subtle, elegant luminosity of the moon. The crescent on her head indicates that the moon is foremost in her thoughts.

Oracle Message

Whatever you are thinking of doing, pay attention to when you plan on doing it. The matter at hand is particularly sensitive to timing. This may be either lunar timing or circumstantial timing. Whichever it is, do pick carefully in order to assure the best possible success.

Moon Time

If you are planning on doing something, use these journal questions to help you determine the best time.

1. Describe what you want to do.

2. What aspect of this would you consider a new beginning of something?

3. What is the role of increasing or growth in this project?

4. Is this something you've already started? If so, how close to completion are you? Is it something that requires a lot of energy?

5. How does the idea of decreasing or banishing play into the plan?

Whatever phase you select, you can enchant your charm to focus the moon's energy to support you in your plan. You can do this enchantment during your selected moon phase or during a full moon.

Carve a circle into a white candle and then add a crescent, like this: ◑. Anoint the candle with either jasmine or ylang-ylang oil (both are associated with the moon's power). Light the candle, and place your charm in front of it. Say this:

> *Goddess of the night*
> *Guide me with wisdom*
> *And your shining light.*
> *I honor you when dark*
> *I honor as you grow*
> *I honor you in fullness*
> *And as you fade and go.*
> *Goddess of the night*
> *Fill me with your wisdom*
> *And this charm with light.*

When you are done, if safe and appropriate, let the candle burn out. If not, snuff the candle. Carry or wear your charm as a symbol of the moon's power that is within you.

MERMAID DREAMS

D o you remember your dreams? Dreams are one way the universe sends messages. But with the blare of the alarm clock, the dream vanishes, and our message is lost.

Every day, we are swamped with communication. These days, we are rarely unavailable. Cell phones with voice mail, texting, and email are common (who can get along without one?). The Internet, TV, and even movie theatres throw messages (usually commercials) at us. Someone always wants to tell us something. With all that chatter, it's no wonder we have a hard time hearing messages from the universe. We know that if we tune in to the flow of the earth and nature, we can find guidance and wisdom to help us in our daily lives. The universe speaks to us in many ways, for example, through our dreams and through our intuition. The trouble is, we usually can't hear it. Or if we do hear our intuition, often we don't trust it. It's easy to discount it. When someone asks why about something, and you say it was "just a hunch," rolling eyes can be the response. We don't always feel confident in our intuition as a means of making decisions. We often feel more comfortable if we have some sort of fact to base it on. But by discounting our dreams and intuition, we miss out on useful information and we sell ourselves short.

This mermaid, lost in the midst of her daydreams, has no trouble whatsoever hearing her intuition or remembering her dreams. She rests calmly on a crescent moon. The moon is, of course, associated with dreams and intuition. Although her eyes are open, she is focused inward. The sea around her is quietly and gently flowing around, just enough to sway and relax her, but not enough to be distracting. Her long hair is laced with strings of pearls, softly white and luminous like the moon, representing all the pearls of wisdom she has gathered in just such quiet moments.

Oracle Message

At this time, pay special attention to your dreams. If you do, you will find messages and inspiration. Keep a dream journal by your bed, so you can write down dreams during the night. You may find the answer to your question, the perfect gift idea for someone, or a design idea for a project you're working on. Heed your intuition as well. The more you use it, the more you will grow to trust it. Your intuition is a great tool. It has access to knowledge that you cannot know with logic and is connected with the flow of the universe. So much awesomeness and brilliance lies hidden there—tap into it!

Dream Enhancement

To enhance your awareness of your dreams, wrap some mint and rosemary in a cloth and tie tightly (or place in a small cloth bag). Put this under your pillow. Wrap the herbs well. Their scents are energizing, so you don't want to smell them when you are trying to sleep.

Intuition Charm

If you want to be more open to intuitive messages, wrap your charm with a moonstone in a silver cloth. Light a white candle, and say three times:

Lady of the moon, wise and bright
You banish darkness from the night
Enchant this charm and let it bring
Your messages about anything.

Snuff out the candle. Place the stone and charm under the light of the full moon (inside on a windowsill, not outside) for one night. Carry the stone and wear or carry the charm to help you be more sensitive to your intuition.

MOTHER EARTH

While we may have jobs we love and that require much of our time and energy, home will always be something else entirely. Home is why we work. And while we may have issues with our families, they are family and somehow stick with us through thick and thin.

A peaceful and stable home life can make it easier to withstand the ebb and flow, the ups and downs, the chaos and catastrophes of activities outside the home. It also provides a place to celebrate life's joys and your accomplishments. How wonderful it is to come home after a long day and feel totally comfortable and safe. Surrounded by loved ones, you know the evening will be enjoyable, filled with sharing and support. When at home, you should be able to be yourself and not worry about playing a role. If you have a place like this to land at the end of the day, it makes everything else much better.

The pregnant Mother Earth depicts nothing more and nothing less than a perfect home and family life. Draped in yellow, the color of the sun and creativity, she stands proudly and confidently with the raven and the stag. She is comfortable around all creatures, and they are at ease with her. Behind her head is a symbol of the earth, with the promise of abundance for all creatures. Within her own body, she nourishes and protects tender and fragile life. This is a goddess of all elements of life who wants a safe place for all.

Oracle Message

You can expect peace, harmony, and happiness at home. If you already have it, learn to let it support and comfort you more than you currently do. This is a place where you can and should draw strength. If you don't already enjoy this blessing, you are probably noticing the lack of it and desire a change. Whatever the challenges or difficulties you faced in the past, the time is here to do what you can to create a better, more nurturing home life. You have the wisdom and ability. The universe is open to it. You are like Mother Earth: you can create the home life you desire.

Cleaning House

If you are less than pleased with your current home life, take matters into your own hands. Apply some magic and a little love, and you'll turn things around in time. If you can have some time home alone, that works best. First, smudge the house with sage, paying attention to corners and doorways. Depending on where you live, plant some rosemary and lavender outside your entrance, or have potted plants in the house near the door. Have a small bowl and a rose quartz for each room. In the bowl, place a little salt for cleansing and a rose quartz for healing and love. Place a bowl out of sight in each room. Finally, starting at the front door, walk through each room and say:

Mother Earth, mother of all
Hear my prayer, heed my call.
Banish discord from this place
Send love and peace to replace.
Mother Earth, mother of all
Hear my prayer, heed my call.

When family members enter, greet them with a hug and a kind word (but you always do, don't you?).

Dream Come True

This journal exercise can help you create your ideal home life with the power of visualization coupled with constructive actions.

Every evening for at least three days (or for as long as you wish), write out a situation or aspect of your home life that you aren't happy with. Describe it as objectively as possible. Write out how you'd like it to be different. Sit back and imagine it as clearly as you can. Come up with one thing that you can do to move in that direction. In the morning, reread your entry and remind yourself to take that one action. Repeat until your home life is so happy that it's like a dream come true—which is exactly what it is.

MYSTIC MERMAID

There are lots of kinds of magic in this world. Sometimes the best magic for the spirit is a little magical attention to the body.

Isn't it interesting how a good meal, an exquisite bit of chocolate, a perfect wine, a song, or a soft bed can lift the spirit? We don't usually think of physical pampering as feeding the soul, but it does. Our bodies are more than containers for souls. They are part of the universe, and just as we honor the sun, the moon, nature, each other, and our own spirits, we shouldn't neglect our bodies. When we feel pampered and cared for, we want others to feel good, too, so we turn our attention very naturally to their needs.

It's a really nice cycle. We make ourselves feel good, then we help others feel good. Then they'll probably spread the good. Oh, and if you are still unsure of the idea of pampering your body for its own sake, don't worry. There are ways that are magical and designed to nourish the spirit as well as soften the skin.

This Mystic Mermaid isn't worried about anything at the moment. She has created her own circle of light. Within that circle, she is delighting in whatever scents she's added to her space, enjoying the flow of water over her body, and treating her sea-worn skin with some soothing oil.

Oracle Message

Quite simply: treat yourself. Pamper yourself in whatever way you can. Have you been considering a full day at the spa? The answer here is, "Do it." And if a full day is out of your budget, or maybe not your style, be creative. You know what you like. A new nail polish or lipstick...an extra hour of sleep on lovely, clean sheets...peppermint essential oil...a bright scarf...an hour alone with a good book and the perfect cup of tea...a stolen afternoon walk in the park...well, you get the idea. When you are done, find a way to send a little pampering someone else's way: a packet of tea you know they'll like, a fancy truffle, a magazine, some scented lotion.

Pampering Body and Soul

Do you keep a journal, a dream diary, or a Book of Shadows? How about keeping a book of what kinds of oils you like, their properties, and how they affect you? Essential oils have magical properties and they have therapeutic properties; they are not always the same. Also, there may be some with the magical quality you are looking for, but you don't like the smell. You will want to keep track of how you react to the scents. Everyone is different. So while mint and rosemary are usually energizing, you may not find them so. Lavender is generally relaxing, but it may not have that effect on you.

As you learn which oils work best for you magically, therapeutically, and personally, you can use them in your own spells and enchantments. And you can use them to pamper yourself with magical intent as well as physical benefits. Experiment with blends. Try balancing something earthy with something light, like sandalwood or patchouli with rose, bergamot, or ylang-ylang. Peppermint is very versatile and works well with lavender, rosemary, lemon, or eucalyptus. Clary sage and lavender is one of my personal favorites.

You can add about fifteen drops of your special blend along with two tablespoons of sweet almond oil to your bath. A few drops blended in unscented lotion will let you enjoy the scent all day. And you can always apply a few drops to your wrists for a more powerful punch.

For a special treat for your hands and feet, add a few tablespoons of olive oil or sweet almond oil to about a cup of salt. Add a few drops of an oil blend that you find either soothing or invigorating (depending on whether you want to relax or revive) to the salt mixture. Rub your feet or hands with it over a sink or foot bath (it's messy). After you've massaged for a few minutes, rub off all the salt. Leave some of the oil behind and rub it into your skin. You'll be soft, clean, and delightfully scented.

With all oils, do remember to check for sensitivity.

NEMESIS

Almost every spiritual path and every political system incorporates the notion of justice. Whatever you do has consequences. If you put out negative energy, you draw negative energy to you.

"You've made your bed, now you have to sleep in it."

"You reap what you sow."

"Every action has an equal and opposite reaction."

"It's karmic payback time."

Luckily, this works both ways, so if you express positive energy, you will attract positive energy. In this way, your past actions have created your present. And you are, with every action, creating your future. This is a law of the universe. It lays the burden of responsibility for your own life firmly at your feet. It also removes a burden of responsibility: you don't need to concern yourself with making someone else pay for their wrongs. The universe doesn't need your help. Understanding this will help you focus on and assess your own choices. Paying attention to the ramifications of your own decisions empowers you to create the kind of future you want.

The Greek goddess Nemesis reflects that society's values and is concerned with divine retribution, punishing pride and unwarranted success. Here, our Nemesis's focus is broader. She represents a more universal type of balance and is better understood as karma, hence the etching on her sword and tattoo near her eye—a kanji symbol for karma. She does not seek merely to right wrongs and punish. Rather, she bestows whatever has been earned, both good and bad. She is a complete and pure expression of justice. Like the Greek image, she is winged. In some myths, she is associated with geese or swans, and so she holds a feather in her hand. She stands before an ancient pagan symbol of justice. She draws her motivation from a sense of justice; she sees where justice needs to be applied; she actively applies justice.

Oracle Message

Whatever you are facing now, positive or negative, is a result of past actions. There is likely no avoiding it. If positive, enjoy it. If negative, assess the decisions and behaviors that may have brought you to this point. Learn from this experience. Also, since you are, at this moment, laying the groundwork for your future, consider carefully how you react in this situation. Will your reactions bring about more of the same, or are you growing in a positive direction?

What Color Is Your Karma?

Alas, there is no spell or enchantment you can do to alter your past karma. Nor should you concern yourself with attending to someone else's karma. Instead, use the journaling suggestions below to help you understand your own karma.

1. Whatever your current situation, review your past actions especially as they pertain to this issue. Make a timeline showing how your actions brought you to this moment. It might be easier to work backward in time.

2. Think of a positive situation you experienced. Repeat the timeline suggestions described above. What can you repeat to create more positive energy?

3. Think of a negative situation you experienced. Repeat the timeline suggestions described above. What will you avoid in the future and why?

4. In reviewing any of the above situations, were there actions you took or decisions you made that had unexpected consequences? Did you do something with the best of intentions that had less than positive results? What happened? What can you learn from it?

5. Are you tempted to mess with someone else's karma in a kind of "I want to hurt them as badly as they hurt me" way? Imagine that you do so. Write out the ramifications, both short- and long-term. How would such behavior shape your future karma?

6. While you don't want to make someone pay for bad behavior toward you, if you let them continue treating you badly, do you have any karmic responsibility for enabling negative energy?

NIGHT QUEEN

Before the world was fully mapped and charted, mapmakers would draw maps of as much of the world as they knew. Beyond the known lands there was shadowy speculation and the warning: beyond here, there be dragons.

We often imagine metaphorical dragons populating the dark, uncharted parts of our lives. Sometimes there are, and sometimes there aren't. Much of the time, we stay where we're comfortable, in familiar surroundings doing familiar things while thinking and feeling familiar thoughts and emotions. At other times, we seek the thrill of the unknown and venture forth bravely. Or we may be thrust, quite unwillingly, into the darkness. However often we move out of our comfort zone, the experiences are always different. We may find ourselves pleasantly surprised, disappointed, enlightened, horrified, or any other feeling, or even a combination. No matter the experience, we return from those forays and our life is never the same again. Whatever we bring back shapes and colors our future experiences.

Some shamans and Native Americans practice a very conscious and deliberate visit to unknown worlds to seek spiritual enlightenment. These vision quests, or shamanic journeys, can be dangerous. While we may not wish to go on a traditional vision quest, we can adapt the idea for our own spiritual journeys.

The Night Queen is about to embark on a journey. She looks back at us to see if we are ready to go with her. While she does not know where she is going, she knows why she is going. She seeks wisdom and is willing to venture into the unknown to find it. She wraps herself in a black cloak, the color of the night, but underneath she is unclothed, a symbol of her vulnerability during this trip. Her companion is a raven who will whisper secrets and messages to help her along. In her hand she carries a key, representing the purpose of her quest: to unlock the doors to mysteries. Guiding her path is the full moon.

Oracle Message

You would benefit from some very conscious spiritual seeking. You are being invited to visit the dark corners of your soul and the uncharted realms of the spirit world. Realize that this is not a pleasurable ramble through the woods, with sunlight spilling through the leaves. Instead, you will be asked to bare your soul and face fears. Questions that make you uncomfortable will demand answers. Parts of yourself that you have hidden will be revealed—and you will have to deal with them. Fun? Probably not, but it is guaranteed to be powerful and transformative.

Into the Dark

During this journey, you will want to stay in close contact with the universe, the goddess, or whatever deity you honor. You will desire guidance with each step. You will need strength along the way. As a symbol of this relationship, enchant your fairy charm and keep it with you.

Do this enchantment during the new or waning moon to symbolize your journey into the dark. Mix together a few drops of clary sage, sandalwood, and rosemary essential oils. Anoint a white candle, and light it. Anoint your charm, and say three times:

> *I call to thee, my guiding light*
> *Walk close to me all through the night*
> *I call to thee, my guiding light.*

My guiding light, I call to thee
So I can face what comes to me
My guiding light, I call to thee.

Wear or carry your charm as a reminder that you are not alone on this journey.

NIGHTFALL

Life is full of cycles. The sun rises and sets. Years begin and end. Seasons come and go. Events or projects are planned, executed, and then completed. Jobs are found and sometimes lost. Relationships that enter your life so full of promise can leave your life.

Beginnings are often filled with joy and hope. Cherish those times. Sometimes we take them for granted. Endings are often permeated with sadness and pain. When things, events, or people leave our lives, they can leave great holes like exit wounds. A mourning period usually follows, where we may wait for that which was lost to return to us. After a while, we realize it will not return, and we mourn the loss. This is natural and must happen before the next phase or cycle can begin.

In Nightfall, a ghostly fairy waits in an empty room before a window. A full moon rises to its throne in a cloudy sky, its sparse light dimmed; shadows overwhelm the landscape. The fairy holds a single candle, a bit of hope, that is of little use in illuminating the darkness that surrounds her. The walls are painted in large, mournful black roses, depicting her sense of lost joy. The bare tree branches symbolize her bleak outlook. She is interrupted from her lonely vigil, as if someone has entered the room, inviting her to return to life. But her sad expression lets us know that she is not ready.

Oracle Message

A tremendous loss or longing casts darkness over your life. It feels as if all the color and joy is gone. You are waiting for its return. Sadly, though, it seems that whatever it is will not return soon. The pain and disappointment must run their natural course. You cannot rush such healing. It is time to stay with your loss, honoring and acknowledging that which is gone. But know this, too: life will beckon again, and you will eventually be able to answer its call and begin your next cycle.

To Honor and Mourn a Loss

Perform this spell during a waning moon to ease the pain and promote healing from a loss. One of the dangers of mourning is to fall too far into it, to become obsessed and not heal. In a small bag or cloth (use either pink for emotional healing or blue for spiritual protection), place a bit of rosemary for remembrance and mugwort to guard against obsession. Close the bag or tie up the cloth to make a bag. Light a black and a white candle in separate fireproof bowls or dishes large enough to safely burn a small piece of paper. Place the bag between the two candles in their holders.

Take some time to think about what you've lost. Think about what you must let go. Write it on a small piece of paper. Think about what you must remember and take with you into the future. Write that on another small piece of paper.

Say the following prayer. Light the first piece of paper with the black candle, and let it burn in the dish or bowl.

I beseech thee, Goddess of Night
Take this pain and this loss from me
I beseech thee: let pain take flight
Take this pain as I honor thee.

Say the following prayer. Light the second piece of paper with the white candle, and let it burn in the dish or bowl.

I thank thee, O Goddess of Night
For this gift and this memory
Let me always keep it in sight
I will remember; so let it be.

Let the candles burn out, if it is safe to do so, or snuff them out. Keep the herb bag under your pillow for one lunar cycle. Then safely burn the herbs, and return the ashes to the earth.

RENAISSANCE ROSE

enaissance means "rebirth" or "revival." It is similar to a transformation, but there is a difference. Revival focuses on bringing back something that was. In the course of bringing something back, that something clearly will be changed because of the passage of time and because we are seeing it with different eyes. It will still retain something of its original nature, but it may be altered. A transformation indicates a more complete change—something turns into something else.

Sometimes things you love pass from your life or you let them go to make way for new things. You may lose interest in a hobby, lose touch with a friend, drop a habit, or stop a particular practice. At some point in the past, those things added to your life. Did they leave your life because they no longer brought you joy? Or was there some other reason? How would your life be different if they didn't leave? What would it be like if they returned?

Our Renaissance Rose fairy invites us to explore the idea of lost and rediscovered love. The red jewels on her headpiece show her intent and focus; she is thinking about things she loves or loved. The rose in her hand symbolizes love. Petals fall from her fingertips, indicating the loss of things that she loved. The moths nearby remind her of changes that occur when something is lost—changes in herself, her life, and the people, things, or activities that are now gone from her.

Oracle Message

There is something from your past, distant or recent, that you've lost. Maybe it moved out of your life quite by accident, or perhaps you consciously moved it out. Whatever it is, it is time to bring it back in some form. There is a hole, a lack of balance in your life, and this is the thing that needs to be there. It may not be exactly the same as the last time it was in your life. Or it may be exactly the same, and it is you who are different. In any event, there will be a comfortable familiarity as well as a magical time of getting reacquainted.

Which One?

If you get this card and you are unsure about what it refers to, use your fairy charm as a pendulum to help you find the answer. If there are several possibilities, write each one on a separate piece of paper. Make sure you know how your pendulum swings for yes and for no before you start. Hold your pendulum over each possibility, asking, "Is this the thing (or person or activity) I should bring back into my life?"

SERENITY

When you find yourself navigating tumultuous waters in your life, it's easy to feel out of control. But imagine yourself literally adrift in a stormy sea. Your instinct, your fear, may cause you to flail about. But that doesn't help, does it? In fact, it usually makes the situation worse, as you wear yourself out and have no energy left to take useful action.

In times like these, you'll want to find your peaceful center, a place where you feel strong and balanced. If you can find this place, you can rise above the tumult and at the very least not exhaust yourself or make the situation worse. At the most, you'll be able to hear the voice in your heart guide you as you seek the best solutions and actions to take.

Clad in white and purple, signifying purity and spirituality, the Serenity fairy stands on a pillar. The strong, intricately carved pillar represents her inner core, her peaceful center. Standing on it, she is able to rise above the tumult and chaos. The power of the full moon, enhancing her intuitive powers, is echoed by the amethyst worn near her heart. The ethereal moths carry to her the sweet, clear voice of the universe, revealing to her the path of peace. The actions she will take become like stars, lights of truth and tranquility, that she pours onto the troubled waters below.

Oracle Message

When facing chaotic or troubled times, there are any number of effective approaches. Sometimes a strong stance is necessary. Sometimes a gentler hand is better. In this case, you are being advised to rise above the situation and seek the council of your heart. Don't waste your energy by fretting, worrying, or becoming angry. Pull back, and ask the universe to show you a peaceful approach. This may also be an opportunity for you to grow spiritually.

Serenity Visualization

It's all very well and good to want to step back, but when our instinct is fight, fret, or flail, it's good to have a plan. Meditation is "stepping back" by its very nature, and it is an ideal way to hear the voice of your heart as you quiet your mind.

Sit comfortably in a chair with your feet on the ground, or lie down, if you prefer, in a room where you won't be disturbed. Close your eyes, and picture yourself on a pedestal over a turbulent sea. If you feel the motion of the waves, imagine yourself standing firmly and calmly on your feet; spread your toes, and feel the cool, strong base of the pedestal. Imagine the moon behind you, and see the light it casts, dancing, over the waves. When you feel balanced, picture yourself raising your arms and asking, with confidence, for serenity and for guidance. Imagine delicate white and purple moths coming to you, whispering gentle messages. Hold the image until you are satisfied that you've received the wisdom you seek. Thank the universe, and open your eyes.

Serenity Charm

If you know the peaceful actions you must take but find the application difficult, a serenity charm enchantment can help you. Take your fairy charm and put it on a purple or a white ribbon. Anoint it with lavender essential oil. Wrap it, along with a rose quartz or amethyst, in silk, ideally white or purple, although any color but black would be fine. Also, a clear quartz will add strength to this charm. Place the bundle on a table, and light a white candle. Allowing

your voice to grow softer and quieter each time, say the
following verse three times:

> *Light of peace, I call on thee*
> *I seek peace, and peace I need*
> *Let me rise above the sea*
> *Fill this charm, my cry please heed.*

Sit quietly for a few minutes, focusing on your desire.
Thank the universe, snuff the candle, undo the bundle,
and tie the enchanted charm around your neck, allowing it
to rest near your heart.

SHADOW WEAVER

When was the last time you felt powerful and in control of your life? Isn't that a great feeling? There can be tons going on, but you've got every ball in the air, every single thing in order, and everything is moving forward in the exact direction you want it to go. Those times may be rare for some of us, but they sure feel good.

And then there are times when we just can't seem to motivate and properly handle one thing, let alone several. Or we might have so much going on that we feel overwhelmed, throw up our hands, and just let everything go. Those times definitely do not feel so great.

Whatever situation we face, we can know that we really do have the ability to handle, and handle well, everything. It may not be particularly fun. There may be other things we'd rather do. But if we control our focus and see it through, afterwards the sense of exhilaration and pride will more than make up for it.

The Shadow Weaver is clearly a powerful creature. She is surrounded by chaotic forces stirred up by a black and a white dragon. She strides strongly and confidently forward, subduing and calming them as she passes. Her red bodice and crescent moon indicate her power, power that she knows is hers deep in her gut and wholly understands in her mind. She wears a choker adorned with a yin/yang symbol, showing her ability to balance a variety of energies. In her hands she carries a black beetle and a white butterfly, representing her ability to focus and use opposing energies as she wishes.

Oracle Message

There is something—or several or even many things—going on in your life. Perhaps you're feeling overwhelmed. Maybe your life appears out of control. Maybe it's just one project that you can't get a grip on. Whichever is the case, this card is here to tell you that letting things fall apart, letting something slide—well, that's just not an option right now. There are times when it is okay, and no harm is done. But now it is in your best interest to tap into your deepest, strongest organizational and "get it done" powers, and use them.

You As the Shadow Weaver

When this card comes up and you have no idea where you are going to find that energy, use this visualization to help you tap into it. It can also suggest practical advice on how to approach the task or tasks.

In a quiet room where you know you won't be disturbed, sit comfortably with your feet on the ground, or lie down, if you prefer. Take a close look at the Shadow Weaver card. Close your eyes. Imagine yourself standing tall and confident. Picture yourself in a red bodice (you know you want to). Imagine the task or tasks that face you as dragons in front of you. The energy surrounding them whips and swirls around you. See yourself through the chaos, lifting your arms and quelling the pandemonium. In the silence that you created, watch yourself stride forward and observing those now-docile dragons with a look that says, "You know who's in charge here."

If you wish to continue the meditation, approach the dragons that represent your challenges and tasks, and ask them, "What does it take to control you?" These conversations may lead to practical answers that will help you focus your energy more efficiently.

Oh No, You Don't

When you feel like everyone and everything is pulling at you, trying to get your attention, sapping your energy... put a stop to it. Create the quiet and the space you need to figure out your plan of action. Since you're already frazzled, this spell is super simple and quick.

In your mind, clearly identify the two (or more) people or situations that are creating all the chaos in your life. Get a candle to represent each one of them. Set them in front of you, and light them. Look at each of them for a moment, then, one after the other, blow them out. Smile. Enjoy the quiet, and make your plan. It's nice to take control.

Silver Moon Fairy

There is a time and place for everything. There is a time to be open, forthcoming, and vulnerable. And there is a time to keep things to yourself.

Words have power. Knowledge is a kind of power. When we have dreams and goals, usually it is a good practice to share these with others. Speaking them out loud gives them energy and the power to become reality. Having others know about them can help motivate us to achieve them. But sometimes dreams or goals are not meant to be shared. Perhaps they are not fully formed in your mind yet; perhaps they are too fragile and someone's negative reaction could adversely affect them. Perhaps they require only your power for a while before they are ready to be spoken. Secrets have their own kind of power.

The Silver Moon fairy knows all about keeping secrets. Certainly she is guarded, with her arms crossed tightly around her, and adorned with crescent moons, showing that much is still unrevealed. However, with her purple and white tresses, we know her intent is for the greater good and stems from a spiritual understanding. She is clothed in black, a color of protection, but draped as well in purple, representing a spiritual reason for the protection. The silver full moon behind her represents wisdom, power, and secrets.

Oracle Message

Now is the time to keep silent. Don't share your plans, dreams, goals, or hopes. For whatever reason, now is the time to guard them closely in your heart. Keep them between you and the universe. Take the time to examine them and make sure they are good. Pray and meditate; seek advice in this way only for now. If all is well, nurture them and plan for them on your own, perhaps in your journal. When time passes or circumstances change, then may be the time to share them with others.

To Keep Silent

Sometimes it is hard to keep something to yourself, especially if you don't fully understand why you need to. But if that is the case, you may want to use your fairy charm as an amulet to remind you to guard your innermost thoughts and feelings for now.

You can work this enchantment during any moon phase, but working it on a Monday will give it an extra boost, because Monday is associated with the moon, mysteries, the goddess, and the colors silver and white, which correspond to the Silver Moon fairy.

Put your fairy charm on a silver or a white ribbon. Anoint it with a bit of jasmine essential oil. Light a silver or a white candle. Lay the charm near the candle, and say three times:

> *In the name of the goddess*
> *By the light of the silvery moon*
> *Enchant this charm with silence*
> *Don't let me speak too soon.*
> *So let it be.*

If safe and appropriate, let the candle burn out; if not, snuff it out. Wear your enchanted charm or carry it in a pocket as reminder to hold your dreams safe.

After circumstances have changed or some time has passed, you may wonder if now is a good time to share your thoughts. You can either ask the *Enchanted Oracle* cards or use your enchanted charm as a pendulum. If you want to use your pendulum (and have already calibrated it so you know how it answers yes and no), hold it and say:

> *In the name of the goddess*
> *By the light of the silvery moon*
> *Is it time to break the silence*
> *Tell me, is it yet too soon?*

Repeat this until you receive your answer. If your pendulum indicates no answer, it may mean that it is okay to share with some people but not everyone. If this is the case, write down the names on separate pieces of paper, and repeat the divination for each name.

SPIRIT OF SAMHAIN

Certain times of the year bring with them their own special magic. Samhain is usually celebrated on the evening of October 31. This time of year, the end of summer and the beginning of the dark season, is recognized by many religions and cultures with holidays such as Halloween, All Hallow's Eve, All Souls' Day, and the Day of the Dead. Samhain began as the Celtic New Year and is now celebrated by Wiccans as the New Year as well.

Samhain's magic is powerful and, to some, a bit frightening. During this time, the door between worlds is opened. The veil between the living and the dead, the past and the future, is at its thinnest. On a more mundane level, it marks the end of the harvest, and as such is an opportune time to give thanks. The end of summer also means the beginning of the dark time, the perfect time to request protection for the short days and long nights ahead.

In the Spirit of Samhain, we see a striking embodiment of the season, appropriately clad in flowing black, her hair swept up by the blustery autumn winds, standing in the doorway between worlds. She is here to guide you as you explore the space between life and death, lightness and dark, your past and your future.

The images of the full and crescent moon show lunar energy, full of mystery and magic. Using this energy, we can connect to the flow of spirit, enhancing our psychic and intuitive powers. The Spirit of Samhain carries a small cauldron of fire. The cauldron itself is a place where transformation occurs, where specific ingredients are changed by the application of fire. The ingredients undergo a death and are reborn into a new substance. Beside her is a pedestal with an apple and a raven. The apple tree has a long history of standing between the worlds. In Druid traditions, a silver bough was cut from an apple tree and used to open the doors between realms and experience a transformative journey. Ravens have a long association with the otherworld, death, regeneration, magic, and omens. This raven is more than a messenger; it is a guide who can take you safely to the boundary between the worlds.

Oracle Message

You are in between life and death—not literally but figuratively. Some aspect of your life is over, and the moment of transformation has not yet come. This place may seem like an uncomfortable limbo. However, you have the opportunity to reach into the realms of the otherworld and gain wisdom that will complete your transformation. Pay close attention to your intuition and omens. The time for magical change is upon you!

The Spirit of Samhain Magic

Part of the ancient Samhain rituals included honoring loved ones who have passed on. Honor one of your departed loved ones by making an offering of a meal. It doesn't have to be a full meal, but a symbolic meal. Invite their spirit. Express your love and gratitude for the gifts they gave during their life. Welcome any wisdom or guidance they may wish to offer you. After the meal, if you have an altar, leave the portion for the departed on it overnight. In any case, when it is time to dispose of the food, return it to the earth by composting or by feeding it to animals.

Because this is the beginning of the Celtic New Year, do a divination for the year ahead, and ask your ancestors to give you a message for each month to guide you through the year ahead.

Samhain Charm

If you have drawn this card and know that you are waiting for a message or omen for guidance but are having trouble receiving it, charge your fairy charm to help you.

On a piece of paper, draw a picture of an apple and a raven (you can cut pictures out of a magazine, if you prefer), leaving enough space between the two to set your charm. Put the paper on a windowsill (on the inside), laying your charm between the images you drew. Leave it there overnight. This is best done during the new moon. The new moon is a time to draw new things into your life, and you are seeking a new message.

Once the charm is charged, wear it or carry it in your pocket to remind you to be open to messages or omens that you might otherwise overlook.

Spirit of Yule

Celebrated on the darkest day of the year, Yule is, first and foremost, a celebration of light. After weeks of successively darker days, it is a time to joyously welcome the return of the sun.

Everything about Yule honors life and light. The Yule log, evergreen trees, bonfires, and candles remind us that life continues even through the darkest times, and that, eventually, the light always reappears. Giving gifts and making merry with friends and family help us remember that no matter how bleak things may appear, there is always something to be thankful for. At this time, people remember the past year and make plans for the upcoming one. Planning for the coming year is a show of faith that we know life will continue on. The birch and oaks may be asleep, but the fir trees and holly adorn the wintery landscape with their life.

The cycle of life is celebrated throughout the year and marked by the seasons and holidays. Our own lives have cycles, too. Just like the waxing and waning of the days through the year and the moon through the months, we experience times of joy and times of sorrow. While no one ever speaks of dying from too much joy, people sometimes feel like giving up during the hard times. Remembering the cycle of life can help us get through our darkest days.

A goddess clad in the colors of life and love holds her baby close. The baby represents the birth of a life, a reason to hope. The dark moon behind her represents the darkness that is leaving to make way for the rising sun. Branches draped in snow represent death, but at their base are fir boughs, a reminder that life is never far away. Red, green, and white candles burn, their glow both a statement of faith about and a celebration of the return of light. In the midst of a grey and empty landscape, she has created a haven to celebrate and nurture life.

Oracle Message

Whether your situation is bleak or just not as bright as you'd like, the Spirit of Yule suggests that you prepare for and call to you the return of light and joy. This is a situation where like things attract. If you actively call forth light and joy, they will come to you. You can do this in many ways, such as focusing on your current blessings and making plans for the time ahead.

Calling the Light

Working with the idea that like attracts like, bring light into your life, no matter what time of year it is. It is best to work in a darkened room where you won't be disturbed. Light bayberry, pine, cedar, or cinnamon incense. Gather as many white, red, green, and gold candles as can safely be lit. Say the following once before lighting each candle:

Darkness, darkness
I banish thee
Love and light
I call to me
With faith I ask
So let it be!

Make a list of all things currently in your life that bring you joy. Roll up the paper, and tie it with a green ribbon. On another piece of paper, write out your plans and hopes

for the next month. Roll it up, and tie it with a red ribbon.
Say the following as you tie both scrolls together with a
gold ribbon:

For each joy, I am grateful
And daily give thanks
For my plans, I am hopeful
And always give thanks.

Put the bundle where you can see it as more light
makes its way to you.

Don't forget to snuff out the candles when you're
finished.

TATTERED DREAMS

We think of "spinning tales" as storytelling. And yet, we do spin more than stories. We each spin our beliefs and experiences into threads and webs that shape the way we look at the world and how we operate within it.

We spin such delicate things as ideas, philosophies, faith, and hope. We believe that what we've made is strong—so strong that we use it as the foundation of our life. It becomes the base from which we operate, by which we make our decisions. Even simple, everyday actions and expectations spring from these fragile webs. You call someone and make plans to meet at a certain time. You expect that person to be there. Why? Well, your web of experience and beliefs about people saying what they mean tells you so. And our beliefs and expectations certainly shape larger things, such as our hopes and dreams. Based on what you believe, you think if you work hard and achieve goals, you will get that promotion. If you do work hard, achieve all your goals, and *don't* get the promotion, how does that affect your web of belief?

Here we see a fairy who is surrounded by ruined webs and threads. Something happened, and everything she's worked on has been affected in some way. Even her powerful wings, which could normally take her up to great heights, are tattered and weakened. Her gloves, which cover her arms, are torn, indicating that whatever she does now is somehow lessened as a result. In her right hand, she holds a rune with the symbol of Mars on it; Mars is a powerful planet that can bring energy both to destroy and to rebuild. On her left hand perches a butterfly, a tiny but potent sign of renewal and rebirth.

Oracle Message

Something that you believed in and counted on has unraveled. A belief has ceased to be true for you anymore. A person has proven false. An outcome has fallen far short of the expectation. Whatever has happened, it has had reverberating effects in your world. It is as if the foundation has been shaken and everything on it has fallen. It is unspeakably distressing, but it has happened nonetheless. It is fortunate, though, that the wheels that create dreams do keep spinning in spite of tragedies. And the same energy that may destroy something can also provide the energy to rebuild. And in the midst of tattered dreams, there is always a butterfly that will give you hope, if only you can see it.

Assessing the Damage,
Finding the Butterfly

After having your beliefs shaken or destroyed, it can be hard to objectively assess the damage or to find hope. Use the questions below to guide you as you journal through this difficult time.

1. Start with the base: what belief specifically was destroyed? Is it a belief specific to one person or institution, or is it a general belief? How did it happen? Why did what happened actually destroy the belief?

2. If specific to a person or institution, has it affected your beliefs about people in general or similar institutions? What other beliefs are affected by this particular one being destroyed? Why and in what way?

3. How is your life going to be different now? Examine all the changes. Will there be positive and negative changes or only negative?

4. Do you know other people who have experienced this or something similar? How did it change them? Do you think the change was beneficial or not? What can you learn from their experience?

5. What new beliefs can fill the hole left by the current loss? Take the time to imagine, one by one, what your life would be like if you implemented each one. Which imagined future is most appealing? Why? Can you live by that belief?

TEMPTATION

As the saying goes, into every life a little temptation comes—sometimes a lot of temptation. It may seem rather innocent. There is that luscious little *something* just sitting there, waiting for the taking. Something so lovely can't be bad, can it? Temptation takes many forms. You can be tempted to partake of something or to do something that you know you shouldn't.

Temptation can be, very simply, something that is outright bad for you. You generally know what these are, and it is a matter of making a smart choice and maybe using a bit of willpower. Temptation can also be taking too much of a good thing. This is a case of exercising moderation. Temptation can also be something that is good in general but is bad or inappropriate for you at this time. Temptation can be subtle, and you may have a difficult time identifying it.

In this card, Temptation looks harmless enough at first glance. A lovely, raven-haired fairy casually offers you an apple. Apples are good, healthy things, yes? Ah, but notice the moon behind her and the shadowy light. Things may not be as they appear. This fairy wears a mask, often a sign that something is being hidden. Even her body language, her arms wrapped tightly about her, clues you in that something is being withheld. Around her waist, she wears a thin sliver of a crescent moon, again showing that there is more hidden than is being revealed.

Oracle Message

Very simply put: resist temptation. Whatever you are facing or considering, whatever someone is offering or encouraging, don't do it. It is possibly outright *not good* for you.

Part of you probably knows that, even if you don't want to admit it to yourself. Or it may seem benign or even good to you, but there is something about it that you don't know. If you knew, if the secrets were revealed, you would agree that it is not the right choice for you.

A Charm to Resist Temptation

You can perform this anytime, but it is even more effective if performed during a full moon. Black is a color that can provide psychic protection, so leave your fairy charm on its black ribbon. Anoint your fairy charm and a piece of tiger's-eye with sandalwood oil. Wrap them in a black cloth, and place the bundle in front of a mirror. Look at your own reflection, with your dominant hand resting on the bundle. Say three times:

> *Resist I can*
> *And resist I will*
> *What is offered*
> *Doesn't fit my bill.*

209

Wear or carry your enchanted charm, and carry the tiger's-eye to remind yourself that you love yourself enough to be strong and resist and that you trust the power of the universe to give you the strength needed.

Cause and Effect

Temptation is by its nature difficult to face. Temptations often appeal to our emotions or instincts. Reason can provide a strong balance and help counteract these emotional or instinctual drives. Use the questions below to guide your journaling.

1. What is the temptation? Describe it in as great a detail as possible. What is most appealing to you about it? What are the benefits?

2. What is the most dangerous thing about this temptation?

3. In what way would this temptation further your life goals? In what ways would it hinder them?

4. If you give in to this temptation, what are the spiritual or ethical ramifications?

5. Are you facing this temptation because you have an unfilled need or desire? If so, are there other, healthier ways that you can meet that need?

6. Imagine you give in. Write out what it would be like, speculating into the future as far as you can, so you can see the long-term ramifications.

7. Imagine that you do not give in. Write out what it would be like. In both this and the previous question, include things that are not directly connected, such as effects on your relationships with others, your spiritual life, etc.

WHITE MAGIC

There are times when our focus is on getting things done, and our energy, if it were a color, would be red, yellow, or orange. Sometimes we are growing or nurturing something, and our energy would be green. When we are in pain or mourning, we may say we're feeling blue, but our energy would look black. If love is filling our lives, then pink is the color of the day.

Magic isn't really colored, but colors are associated with magic and do have power. How do we use white magic or energy? Many people associate it with peace, harmony, and healing. All of us have times in our lives when we need healing, be it physical, spiritual, mental, or emotional. Depending on the severity of your pain, the services of a professional may be called for, not an oracle (no matter how otherwise useful said oracle may be).

That said, there are cases where you can find healing, peace, and comfort on your own or from those close to you. Also, there are times when you will be called on to provide healing or to restore harmony.

Our White Magic witch represents the ability to heal and find the serenity that lives in all of us. She is draped in white and purple, the colors of spirituality, purity, and power. She wears a pentagram at her neck, a sign of the dominion of spirit over the earthly elements. Her white candles shine the light of peace and goodness against the darkness of discomfort and evil. Shimmery drops of light fall from her hair. The pale moths represent the transformative effects of healing power.

Oracle Message

You or someone you care about is in pain. This card brings with it the power and promise of healing and peace. However dark and uncomfortable it has been, a soothing, gentler time approaches. This card can also represent you in the role of healer or peacemaker. If you find yourself called to help someone else, answer that call. If you focus on the center of white magic within your soul, you'll be able to make a difference in someone's life.

Healing Waters

If you are in need of some healing or peace-restoring magic, here is a simple technique. Draw a warm, comfortable bath. Mix a few drops of lavender essential oil with two tablespoons of sweet almond oil, and add them to your bath. Light a purple and a white candle (more, if you have them and it's safe). As you relax in your bath, lie back and close your eyes. Visualize a soft white light filled with a soft, soothing scent and gentle music. Imagine it envelops you, gently supporting your body, easing your senses, quieting your mind. Stay in that safe, healing embrace for as long as you like—or until your bath water gets chilly.

To carry healing or peaceful energy with you, anoint a white ribbon with a drop of lavender as you say:

Heal my body, feed my soul
Feeling healthy is my goal.

Tie the ribbon around your wrist or ankle.

SHINE BRIGHTLY

Magical energy is everywhere and available to everyone. Miracles happen. Deities hear and respond. Life is an amazing journey.

Both Jessica and I hope that this book, these cards, and the fairy charm provide ways for you to access and implement magic in your life. Use these items wisely.

Explore your connections to the past and to nature. Celebrate your glory and your uniqueness. Acknowledge your power. Be beautiful, and be kind.